GUSTAV MAHLER:

HIS MIND AND HIS MUSIC

GUSTAV MAHLER:

HIS MIND AND HIS MUSIC

Volume I

by

NEVILLE CARDUS

*with music examples
copied, written and edited
by Rudolf Schwarz*

VICTOR GOLLANCZ LTD

LONDON · 1965

TO

OTTO KLEMPERER

Printed in Great Britain by
The Camelot Press Ltd., London and Southampton

CONTENTS

ACKNOWLEDGMENTS

I HAVE WRITTEN this book for my own pleasure and have learned something during the course of putting it together. My thanks are due to several friends who have directly or indirectly helped and encouraged me.

First of all, I owe a debt which can never be estimated in its value, and certainly can never be paid, to Rudolf Schwarz, who has not only edited my musical examples but has copied them out, in beautiful hand-written script.

I have found guidance, information and enlightenment in Paul Bekker's *Gustav Mahlers Sinfonien* (Schuster & Loeffler, Berlin, 1921); Richard Specht's *Gustav Mahler* (Schuster & Loeffler, Berlin, 1913); H. F. Redlich's *Bruckner and Mahler* (J. M. Dent & Sons, Ltd, 1955); *Gustav Mahler: The Early Years*, by Donald Mitchell (Rockcliff, London, 1958); Alma Mahler's *Gustav Mahler: Erinnerungen und Briefe* (Albert de Lange, Amsterdam, 1940); *Erinnerungen an Gustav Mahler:* Natalie Bauer-Lechner (Tal Verlag, 1923); Bruno Walter's *Gustav Mahler* (Hamish Hamilton, 1958); *Chord and Discord*, publication of the Bruckner Society of America.

There is also Samuel Langford to remember, my Principal on the *Manchester Guardian*, who opened my ears and mind to the music of Mahler some forty years ago at a time when Mahler was either scarcely a known name in Great Britain, or a composer generally misunderstood.

I should include amongst these grateful acknowledgments Mrs Lili Williams, Mrs Sandra Moss and Miss Livia Gollancz for devoted work on the typescript.

LONDON 1964.   N. C.

ARTIST AND MAN

I

To UNDERSTAND AND get to the heart of Mahler's music calls for an unusual approach. Much of his representative work will not give up its secret if we regard it wholly as music which we can study for its own sake. There is, of course, plenty in Mahler to appeal to us independently as music.

We can think of most compositions as having been born in labour by imagination, nurtured and shaped by selective art, then, as though by the cutting of an umbilical cord, sent into the world, there to live or perish according to their fitness to survive as music. It is not uncommon to hear that a composer has actually disowned a work of his own creation. And there is a whole school of criticism, a righteous school, which condemns an interpretation of music that refers to the composer's life or history, emotional or other. His music is examined by this school as a production *sui generis*, a thing in and by itself to be responded to strictly *qua* music.

It is the fact, indeed, that most compositions are best left to speak for themselves. No really necessary light is likely to fall on a symphony of Beethoven, Mozart, Brahms or Vaughan Williams if we submit any of them to a psychological probing of brain-cells, emotional tensions and so on, as implied by their different kinds of tone-speech. But with Mahler music was a manifestation of the whole man. In music he found his only way of living an uninhibited emergent life. It is hard to separate in abstract thought a symphony by Mahler from our conception of Mahler the man, as he existed, nerve blood and brain, during his periods of gestation. I do not feel when I listen to Beethoven, Bach, Bruckner or Sibelius that I am coming into a sort of psychic contact with the men behind the music. I recognise their tone, their style and technical set-up, the idiom and so on; but I do not get a sense of a personal flavour, a personal presence. With Mahler, his music seems as though it is being projected or ejected from his very being, from his innermost nature, even as we are listening to it in performance. It comes to us at times as a kind of ectoplasm of tone. I can almost see it moving. I have known people made sick by the sound of Mahler. It appears often to take form as it goes on and on, directed by an urge not always farseeing. The music of Mahler might well suggest that it is generated and has its being in much the same way that Mahler himself was propelled by the life-force, from boyhood to a manhood cut short at the age of fifty-one, developing, striving and surviving by trial and error, influenced by tendencies from the parent stock and, once out of the womb, very much at the mercy of chances and vicissitudes of growth and adaptation. Obviously we are not free to apply the ordinary musical tests when we consider the Mahler symphonies, each composed as much from psychological as musical needs. Mahler was not a composer who thought first of fidelity to his medium. He used music to express himself, realise himself as experiencing mind, nature and spirit. So, from this point of view, we cannot with relevance denounce as faults features in Mahler's music definitely questionable in music of a more absolute kind. If, for instance, Brahms had 'carried on', gone off at a tangent in a development section, we should have been justified in raising our eyebrows. If these features in Mahler are perceived by us as the setbacks, frustrations and short-circuitings of a composer for whom music is primarily a means whereby he is seeking integration as man and artist, even during the act of creation—very well, we shall not judge him for what he is not mainly aiming at. In other words, we are not always dealing in Mahler with self-sufficient musical entities, each conceived in more or less tranquil recollection and consistently controlled by craftsmanship until conception has been formalised once and for all. With Mahler, one symphony begets another; as we study we are dealing with psychological growth and change. He was not the perfect artist ready to submit to law and limitations of music. He did not present a symphony to us as though saying: 'There—admire it or dislike it as a symphony, complete in itself.' He said that no later work of his could be understood by anybody who had not lived through all its predecessors. The question inevitably comes up: is it worth our while to explore all these long, these very long symphonies, if the main content is egocentric, with but one halfpennyworth of music to an intolerable deal of Mahler? Perhaps we shall see.

Here it should be made clear that I am not arguing that Mahler composed empirically, with the hit-or-miss methods of one not a technical master. Mahler's technique and musical equipment were the most extensive and most cultured of his period. The vocal writing and instrumentation of his song-cycles, *Lieder eines fahrenden Gesellen* and *Kindertotenlieder*, are fastidiously stylish. The composer of the 'Symphony of a Thousand', the Eighth, lampooned by a German *New Yorker* of the day—

Trommeln, Becken, Schell'n, Posaunen,
Donnerblechzeug und Kartaunen,
Rathausglockenspielgehämmer,
Löwenbrüllen, Schrei der Lämmer[1]

could relax to the plane of miniature. The orchestration of *Das Lied von der Erde* is often silver-pointed; the song-speech in the 'Abschied' of the same work is fine and subtle in colour and inflection, notable at the phrases:

1

Die Sonne scheidet hinter dem Ge - bir - ge.

and

2

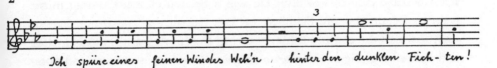

Ich spüre eines feinen Windes Weh'n, hinter den dunklen Fich - ten!

Here music evokes, as beautifully as any I know, the hush and breath of expectancy.

On the other hand, in the symphonies which are more Faustian in energy and aspiration than *Das Lied von der Erde* and the Fourth, Mahler time after time, disturbs musical equanimity and taste. There is the explosion into the Finale of the First Symphony, followed by a fury of whirling strings and assertively mounting brass urged by sheer force to a climax that is out of proportion to the main style of the work, charming and alluring until now. There is the sudden frenzy after the opening funeral march of the Fifth Symphony (*Stürmisch bewegt*). We must be quick to learn, as we listen to Mahler, to prepare for the worst at a prompting in the score marked this way, or *Mit grösster Wildheit;* even the German language fails to indicate by half the ensuing eruptions, drum-cracks, sequential paroxysms of string figuration in a congested yet eddying counterpoint. I do not know in all symphonic music any passages less

[1] From some satirical doggerel in the German comic paper *Meggendorfer Blätter,* more or less untranslatably likening the tone effects of Mahler's voluminous scoring in the Eighth Symphony to all sorts of rackets, including the roaring of lions and the screams of terrified sheep.

musically composed than Mahler's volcanic disturbances, and the reckless rhythmical persistence which recurs, especially in the long-drawn-out Finale of the Sixth Symphony. Yet, in this same Sixth Symphony will be found the closest thematic integration and evidence of fine thinking.

Now Mahler was civilised enough in his art to know as clearly as any of his critics when he was putting on to his manuscript paper an orchestral cliché or a merely physically worked-up crescendo. My theory is that he made miscalculations of tone and dynamics, and suffered subsidences into noisy craters of resonant vacancy, because often he was temporarily removed by his dæmon from the calm detached pivotal-spot from which a composer who is musician first and last never lets himself be shifted. Mahler most times used the materials of music not as composers normally use them, but solely for exploration of his psychological condition at the moment. Now and again the art of music could not contain him, at any rate not in the forms and expressive powers of his period. There were irreconcilable elements in him. He was a belated classic. Coming in the train of Beethoven and Schubert he was palpably a 'romantic'; he was also, towards the end of his life, pointing the future path for Alban Berg and Schönberg. He is today a much more 'modern' sounding composer than, say Brahms or even Wagner.

He looked backward and forward. The Eighth Symphony's first move-ment is a masterpiece of vocal polyphony set to a Latin hymn dating from A.D. 776-856. *Das Lied von der Erde* was described by Ernest Newman as the swan-song of nineteenth-century romanticism in music. The contra-dictions or ambivalence in his music are simply part and parcel of his nature. So closely, indeed, were his experiences of life and the art of musical creation in him bound together that he declared he would be unable to compose at all given peace and tranquillity. ('So sehr ist bei mir Schaffen und Erleben verknüpft, dass, wenn mir mein Dasein fortan ruhig wie ein Wiesenbach dahinflösse, ich—dünkt mich—nichts Rechtes mehr machen könnte').[1] Yet, though he was at the extreme of the 'absolute' composer who can unfold his genius within the recognised scope of his art, in fact drawing inspiration from the material as he fashions it, Mahler was proud to assert that he was first a musician. At any moment he would write and publish a descriptive programme for one of his symphonies, then withdraw it. He said: 'Just as it seems trivial to me to

---

[1] 'So much with me is the creative act and actual experience one and the same, that when I am at peace in my normal being I cannot create anything worth while at all.'

compose to a preconceived programme, I find it unsatisfactory to add one to an existing work.' But he also said: 'When I conceive a composition I always arrive at a point where I must employ the word as bearer of my musical idea.' He tried to make himself consistent and logical on this point by arguing that 'my music arrives at a programme as its last clarification, whereas in the case of Richard Strauss the programme already exists as a given task'.

The difference went deeper. Strauss, in his symphonic poems, set out to describe or portray events and individuals of the visible external world. If Mahler refers by a theme or rhythmical figure to the everyday universe it is not to put us in mind of a particular scene or character but to symbolise some idea or impression felt first within his musical imagination; for example, the trumpet calls in the Second Symphony or the hammer blows in the Sixth. Even the cuckoo calls of the First Symphony are not intended as imitative—they are written in fourths—but to evoke by association the glance back to youth and the Heimat. Mahler was too much the introvert to compose musical inventories of the passing show of the world. He was essentially a religious man, who in music sought strenuously to justify the ways of Mahler not only to God but to himself.

If Mahler had attempted programme music in the Straussian manner, he would probably have made the windmills in *Don Quixote* a symbol of his own varying changes of temperature and feeling. There is no literal pictorialism in Mahler. It is a gross mistake to imagine that Mahler can be listened to mainly in terms of emotional, romantic and extra-musical responses. Though every phrase in Mahler is as a nerve of him, or a brain-cell; though every dynamic variation is a sign of variation of pulse and blood-pressure, none the less all is conveyed to us in music, in tone structure and tone language. We must learn this language, the formulae by which he tries to clarify himself, his psychological states and problems, as he seeks all the time for solution and salvation.

II

Gustav Mahler was born in Kalisch on 7 July 1860 in the Bohemia of the Austrian Empire of Franz Joseph. His father, a Jew, was a coachman who elevated himself with a pathetic class-consciousness to a semi-bourgeois level as proprietor of a dubious sort of distillery. Extant photographs present him holding a top-hat symbolically. He married Marie Frank, daughter of a soap manufacturer. There was little love lost between man and wife; but they produced a dozen offspring, by habit or custom. Five died early, a sixth survived as long as thirteen years, then succumbed, like Mahler himself years later, to a heart weakness. A sister perished young of a tumour of the brain. Brother Otto, who had the makings of a musician in him, committed suicide in his early twenties. Brother Alois fled to America to escape his creditors. Sisters Justine and Emma lived long enough, and normally enough, to provide some domestic stability in Mahler's formative years after the death of his parents when he was twenty-eight. His father, with all his faults, had sense enough to let Gustav study in the Conservatory of Vienna.

But the family as a whole was a living Mahler symphony. Needless to say (needless, really!) the psycho-aestheticians have discovered in Mahler's infancy and home all the main causes of the musical wrath to come: causes of the supposedly dominant note in Mahler's music of a pathological state, of constant and morbid exhibitionism, and all the rest. No doubt most of us as children are fathers of the man, according to our cradle and home; but genius and its ways are not as easily accounted for and foreseen as all that. Mahler himself went into the witness-box on behalf of the clinical method of criticism by submitting himself for examination to Sigmund Freud, in August 1910. (He died in May 1911.) Inevitably a mother-fixation was diagnosed. The more I read of biographical studies today the more I applaud Steinbeck's remark: 'I wish some writer or other artist would be positive and say he did it all himself and his mother wasn't responsible at all.'

Child Mahler, one day caught in a brutal scene between his father and mother, rushed out of the house and ran into an organ-grinder playing 'O du lieber Augustin'. Mahler in his maturity persuaded himself to think that an association in his music of trivial tunes with tragic circumstances was probably a consequence of this far-off incident; he actually argued that it handicapped his development into a great composer. I am prepared to argue that if the incident had any lasting effect on him at all, as mature man and musician, it influenced him to advantage. Many of Mahler's fine strokes of irony in his symphonies are made by contrasts of trivial and sombre tones and rhythms.

But Mahler's most durable music is not perpetually haunted by spectres of the past. It is not perpetually neurotic, dripping with sentimental self-pity, and weak-kneed from too much nostalgic yearning for the cloud-cuckoo land of a happy childhood never experienced. Of his ten completed symphonies, the First, Second, Fifth, Seventh and Eighth end in a defiant 'yes-saying' to life. The Third and the Fourth are in parts as smiling and friendly as though blessed by Schubert and Haydn. I am at a loss to explain why the Fourth Symphony does not share the world's affection for, say, Dvorak's 'New World': it is a symphony of melodic, harmonic, rhythmic, orchestral and vocal enchantments. The final movements of the Fifth and Seventh Symphonies are quite riotously robust revellings in rondo-form. In the *Adante amoroso* of the Seventh Symphony, Mahler is as melodically alluring, as aromatic as Tchaikovsky at his most sensuous; and he is much subtler. Admittedly Mahler escaped from his dæmon only intermittently. None the less it is a mistake to think of him as a psycho-analytical case-book. Genius can't be as easily diagnosed and classified as all that, with the end seen in the beginning. The mind of the creative artist withdraws to an inner environment, a habitat nourished from contact with other minds. The imagination has its own territory and fastnesses; its own laws of growth. New roots have come from soil fertilised by cultures not definable by psycho-analysis, cultures intuitively found by the antennae of genius. Much is made, and rightly, of the influence on Mahler the composer of remembered echoes from the tone-world of his infancy; bugle calls from the neighbouring barracks, bird calls, vistas of the Iglau landscape, grotesque noises in the night-wind. None of the *Mahlerisch* characteristics of mingled nostalgia and naïve spectral evocation are to be found in the Eighth Symphony or in *Das Lied von der Erde*, two masterpieces I would certainly take a risk to save in a general burning of Mahler's output.

The spirit of delight came to him undoubtedly, if only rarely. In these days he is not likely to be considered any the worse for that. He was not complacent, seldom if ever *gemütlich*. That is why young people of our 1960s are finding in him easy lines of approach. He is even modern in feeling. He can be as uncomfortable as the angriest young man. I think that the crisis in the first movement of the Ninth Symphony, culminating in E flat minor *glissandi* in the harps and chromatic triplets in the trombones and horns, is as 'modern' in its terrible menace as any music of today well could be.

Mahler's imagination and art went through strange metamorphoses, not equalled in many other composers. No essential fingerprint to be found in the First Symphony is to be detected in the Eighth, yet the flavour and presence of Mahler are unmistakable in both. For the life of me I cannot understand those of his critics who say that Mahler's music is derivative and reminiscent of other composers. There is a Bruckner tone and idiom (for a brief period) to be heard in the Finale of the Seventh Symphony, and sometimes we are here and there conscious of a Schubertian refrain in the early works. But any familiar tune or rhythm is changed after it has passed through another and powerfully personal mind. 'God Save the Queen' would sound vastly different after, say, Mahler and Berlioz had subdued the tune to their own ways of musical feeling and treatment. There is a special hell waiting for critics who go about hunting for resemblances in different composers and calling them 'borrowings' or even plagiarism. Mahler would have given himself away merely by orchestrating a common chord. In each of his symphonies he goes through a fresh imaginative experience, and comes out modified if not clarified in technique and as a vessel of human consciousness. 'I see everything', he wrote to Bruno Walter, 'in a new light and am in such continuous fluctuation that I shouldn't be surprised if I acquired a new body. I am thirstier than ever for life.' His next symphony might not be an improvement or an advance, judged aesthetically, on its predecessor; but the composer has changed in his metabolism. Mahler needed to have symphonies, much as a woman craves for children, at the risk of producing masterpieces or far from masterpieces.

From the early songs to the rhetorical tragedy-laden Sixth Symphony is as marvellous a transition in style and conception as Wagner's, from *Rienzi* to *Parsifal*. In the *Jugendzeit* songs the melodies are so fresh and lilting at times that Brahms thought that some of them could pass for genuine folk music. The typical melody of Mahler's maturity rises slowly and deliberately on the interval of a third or fourth. When it leaps upward it sustains altitude by a vehement reiteration of the same figure; and sometimes it maintains elevation only by a clinging sort of *gruppetto* or *appoggiatura*. But, as I say, we must not overrate the significance in a great composer of fingerprints. Purely technical mannerisms in music—and after all the so-called fingerprint is rightly so described—tell us nothing of the mind's development. The metamorphosis of Mahler from the *Wunderhorn* symphonies, redolent of the Styrian landscape and *Heimat*, to the austere religious tone and style of the first part of the Eighth Symphony cannot be accounted for in terms of a fingerprint of a fourth, or by any theory of a logical development of style and musical rationale. The change was one of an experiencing genius now protean enough to go into another dimension of imagination. Only by living intensely within himself, and after much wear and tear of mind and spirit, can such changes happen to an artist. We are never unaware of Mahler's presence even through all the liturgical vocal polyphony of the first part of the Eighth Symphony. In the second part, when Mahler is coping with Goethe's symbols of Catholicism as he sets the closing scenes of Part II of *Faust*, the Mahler *Schmalz* is tasted in occasional suave curves of operatic melody and harmony, especially when—of all places—the *Mater Gloriosa* hovers and circles, while violins draw the sweets out of luscious phrases, accompanied by harp and harmonium. By sheer sincerity this music prevails in its context, notably at the movement's and the symphony's end, where the first phrase of the melody is interpolated sequentially into the wonderfully apt setting of Goethe's verses: 'Alles vergängliche'.

Then follows another remarkable change of direction, imaginative and technical, in Mahler's creative history. In his next work, *Das Lied von der Erde*, he went into a tone-world of which there is no prophecy at all in any of his preceding works. The strenuous assertion of faith, choired in the 'Symphony of a Thousand' in terms half-archaic, half-eremitic, has no echo in *Das Lied*. The evocation from Chinese poetry has an intoxicating fatalism, with melody as intimately nuanced in the valedictory section as any in existence. Here are arabesques of instrumentation in a texture of silver grey, the solo voice saying farewell out of orchestral vacancy. Mahler never heard *Das Lied*; it is one of the miracles of creative imagination that such sounds, haunting and drowsy with a submission quite aromatic, should have been conceived within the silent storehouse of a genius's brain.

III

Mahler, more than any other composer, was subject to fits and starts as man and artist. As Bruno Walter has written, 'He never found deliverance in his agonised effort to find sense in human life. He was distracted by ardent activity; he was helped by his humour to cast off the burden. A vivid concern about intellectual questions strengthened him and helped to still a really unquenchable thirst for knowledge and comprehension. Yet his spirit never knew escape from the torturing question: For What? It was the driving impulse of his every activity.' It is vain to try to put into the usual musical categories a composer who was never, or not until nearly too late, integrated into an artist pure and simple, or a composer as such. He used music egocentrically; selfishly, if you like. He can be called creator of the exhibitionist symphony. Maybe music as generally thought of and sought after is not enriched, as art, by a treatment as personal as Mahler's. The vitality of every living note is that of the spirit of Mahler enshrined within. Few stretches of his music, no matter how many good musical qualities they have independently, can be heard for long before they put the question: 'What is it? What is he saying? Why that sudden modulation, why that complete change of tone and direction?'

Mahler's symphonies are sometimes grouped into three periods. Mahler himself made this division: those redolent of the *Wunderhorn* poetry, the First to the Fourth; the purely instrumental Fifth, Sixth and Seventh, supposed—notably by Mahler's most authoritative disciple Bruno Walter—to be 'purely symphonic'; and the Eighth, *Das Lied*, and Ninth, the swan-song, the third group, a period of *Verklärung*, a summing-up.

Mahler, as receiving-set of life's wave-lengths of experience, seems to have had from youth to the year of his death much the same abnormal super-sensitive awareness. Also he was from beginning to end subject to much the same oscillations, short-circuitings. The texture, psychological and musical—with Mahler the terms are usually interchangeable—of the Finale of the First Symphony is as maturely *Mahlerisch* as the second section of the first movement of the 'purely symphonic' Fifth in its strenuous effort to make articulate some inward striving of spirit. And exactly as the hard rhythmic stress and acrid orchestral tone of the First Symphony's Finale melts into *Schmalz* in the forty-six bars (*sehr gesangvoll*) of the contrasted episode, so in the Fifth Symphony Mahler softens to the idealised sentimentality of the Adagietto, where melodic *Schmalz* is refined by his own secret of Neapolitan-sixth modulation.

He was continually revising his scores, not for want of musical art. Not even Strauss was a more cultured and practised master of instrumentation than Mahler. Music, indeed, could not contain his genius, so complex and variegated. He was restless in the world, a split personality. 'I am thrice homeless: as a native of Bohemia in Austria, as an Austrian among Germans, and as a Jew throughout all the world.' He not only struggled with his own musical conceptions but also with the conceptions of other composers. Let us suppose that Toscanini, besides his activities and renown as a conductor ranging over two worlds, had composed in his spare time ten symphonies! This was Mahler's achievement; and he lived some thirty years less than Toscanini. His music has actually been dismissed as 'conductor's music'. Romain Rolland wrote of Mahler's 'assimilations': 'Beethoven taking lessons from Mendelssohn; Chabrier giving Bach a helping hand.' There is not a bar in Mahler that is not at first hearing as unmistakably his own as a living man's voice. He has been related to Beethoven because he used the symphony to express an ethic of humanity. He has been related to Bruckner for much the same reason. He has been linked to Berlioz on the strength of supposedly romantic and picturesque enlargement of symphonic shapes. He has, moreover, been associated with Schubert because now and again his music echoes nature sounds through tone of horn, and *Ländler* rhythm. Mahler was the egoist *par excellence*, which puts him out of the company of Beethoven, Bruckner and Schubert. Berlioz, French romantic capable of a Vergilian objectitivity and dry-eyed pathos—no composer could be psychologically less kin than Berlioz to Mahler.

The Bruckner and Mahler connection, as I shall point out in more detail later, goes no deeper than surface. Each lived in Vienna, and Mahler, though he was not strictly a pupil of Bruckner, admitted that Bruckner's ideals probably had influence on him. Here again, the psychological difference between the two men is great enough to be mutually exclusive. Bruckner rested confidently in the Lord; he found his God without having to hunt him out desperately. By sheer force, not to say by tonal mountain-climbing, Mahler caught a glimpse of a heavenly city at the climactic end of his Eighth Symphony, only to lapse in *Das Lied* into a quietist semi-Oriental fatalism. But he was never the debilitated pessimist. The submission at the end, in the closing Adagio of the Ninth Symphony, as with the beatific bowing-of-the-head at the end of the Adagio of the unfinished Tenth, is not nervous exhaustion; it is acceptance, almost signifying fulfilment. Serenity, even at the end, visited Mahler but intermittently, though there is a foretaste of it in the Adagio of the Third Symphony. Not until we come to the slow movement of the Ninth do we hear in Mahler a warmth of close harmony and a diction telling of some relaxation of mind. Even here, the old tensions, the high blood-pressure of strenuous upward-leaping strings and straining *appoggiature*, break out. He was sufficiently a musical craftsman, consummate master of technique and every symphonic style, to have been equal to composing a continuously temperate Adagio, had he composed mainly as musician.

B

As we have noted already, he was often uneasy about his scores. Had he got down the right tones, the right language? His music is frequently maintained in its course by constant variation—second thoughts! He listened to them with the inner ear, which heard them as they were being conceived, an ear attentive to promptings from Mahler the metaphysical, the didactic searcher, who could at one and the same time indulge the ironic denying spirit and catch overtones of the chorus invisible.

IV

Mahler went so far as to maintain that 'the most important part of music is not in the notes', which is a view of music at the extreme of that of the systematic serial composers. And it is paradoxically because there is more in Mahler's notes than meets the eye or ear that he must be listened to with all possible musical concentration. We are seldom free to sit back during a Mahler symphony and take for granted a stretch of, say, development or recapitulation. There is little pattern-music in Mahler, no formal marking time, no relaxations while he changes key according to custom. Not that he was protean as harmonist, or slave to modulation for its own sake. On the contrary, at his ripest he was mainly contrapuntal, the harmony a by-product of parts having independent motive power. In the instrumental symphonies, the Fifth, Sixth and Seventh, Mahler's melodic lines contend against each other so starkly that they do not blend readily within the give-and-take limits of polyphony. In spite of the numerous instrumental forces often called for in the Mahler orchestra, in spite also of recurrent tonal explosions of the timpani, the texture in general of Mahler has a clearness and litheness which by themselves set him apart from most German and Austrian music. Seldom does he carry too much flesh on his bones; seldom is there any of the unctuous sonority which comes of too much doubling of instrumental parts. There is a certain nervous 'tic' in Mahler, which in itself removes him from the comfortable gemütlich air and bloodstream of music of Teutonic origin or derivation.

The insistent demands Mahler makes on the musical ear, while he is explaining himself and the universe in his own way, are the consequence of his sudden conflicts of nerves and mood, threatening disruption of the symphonic balance which is held together only after a gathering emphasis and tightness of rhythm. Themes breed themes; the length of a Mahler symphonic movement is dictated by the extent of the basic material.

Mahler's themes are seldom spatially compact. A single statement might run to a group of themes, each calling for treatment or partial treatment in the development section. Mahler's extended expositions are supposedly further evidence of his debt to Bruckner; but the method of diffuse or comprehensive statement is entirely natural to Mahler, who always had much to say in a way mingling impulse and intellect, rushes of blood to the head, and reverie logical as a sermon.

His music seems sometimes to expose his nerves. It erupts without warning, after quiet and composedly musical periods. He was wrought in the extreme, a poet realising himself in nature tones, an orchestral rhetorician, a tub-thumper of the timpani, an isolated soliloquist, a sharp thinker—one of the finest brains music has ever known—a tearer of passion to shreds, a romantic of his period, a neo-classic sometimes near the company (as far as aspiring emulation goes) of Beethoven, a forward-looking composer tearing the veil and catching glimpses of the music of to-morrow. Nineteenth-century in his diction and attitudes (faintly 'ham'), yet he is the restless, unanchored man of the twentieth century, not complacent if not angry, not of the bourgeoisie formed by, say, Mendelssohn, Schumann, Brahms, Wagner, Strauss, Elgar. In the Sixth Symphony's first movement, he storms the classic citadel of the symphony, is repulsed in furious disarray, returns to the fight and is thrown back, again in chaotic instrumental disorder. Next moment he escapes to ghostly distant nocturnal haunts. In the endings of the Ninth Symphony, and of the opening slow movement of his Unfinished, the battle is over, the spirit worn and weary. He goes to a cadential grave of resignation. 'Zur Ruh.'

Such was the man who revealed himself without reserve in his every note or group of notes. He has been misunderstood perhaps more than any other composer. It has been suggested (Oxford History of Music, Vol. VII) that his music reveals an orchestral producer rather than a composer. Today he is gaining recognition among young musicians, perhaps for reasons Mahler might not approve. He would wish us to listen to his music for its own content and technique, not for 'influences' or signposts pointing out directions for Schönberg, Alban Berg, Britten, Shostakovitch, and the rest. His own extraordinary gravitations from the tonal centres, regarded in his day as eternally rooted, were the consequence of some piercing of his inner imaginative ear, not of systematic inquiry.

He was first written of with knowledge and insight in this country by

Samuel Langford, critic of the *Manchester Guardian*, who in 1920 found
an essential clue to one of the Mahler secrets:

'In his early songs, which were set with orchestral accompaniment
to folk verses from *Des Knaben Wunderhorn*, both the melodies and
the instruments were imagined in the terms of the country life he had
left.

'This life remained the light of all his seeing. When he came to write
his symphonies, he took again those snatches, instrumental and vocal, of
these orchestral songs, and made them, in more or less obvious allusion,
the key to his poetic and musical feeling. He never entirely separated
instrumental from the vocal imagination in music.'

Langford's view on Mahler might be challenged by those of his admirers
who claim that his Fifth, Sixth and Seventh symphonies are entirely
instrumental in character, to be listened to *qua* symphony. But the
Scherzo of the Fifth is a mature reminiscence of old *Wunderhorn* flavours
of *Ländler* happiness. And in the Seventh Symphony, the echoes of
Wunderhorn macabre are heard in the second movement, echoes of the
song 'Revelge', grisly yet alluring with strains of disembodied midnight
marches. In the Seventh Symphony's Rondo Finale, where Mahler is
without poetic stimuli, he is reduced to music-making pure and simple.
Frankly, he is at a loss for fresh ideas; he has exhausted his resources as a
master of *durchkomponiert* form, and as a composer who, however gifted,
was much less and much more than a composer.

He was sometimes a vain little man. When he was director of the
Vienna Court Opera certain singers knew how to get round him—and
Toscanini was never more vehemently jealous of standards than Mahler,
the fanatical idealist. One of these singers, wishing a favour, waited to
catch Mahler on his way home down the 'Renngasse. He passed him
singing a theme from a Mahler symphony. Mahler recognised him,
almost embraced him, crying out, 'You know my music! You know my
music!' Not a question but an exclamation of gratification. The singer
got what he wanted of Mahler, straightaway.

Is this a story showing Mahler as a small man? I think not; it is rather
touching. A truly vain man would take for granted that any musician
worth the name would know his music. Mahler had a sense of his own
inferiority; his music expresses it. He wrote few flawless, fully-realised

works of large size. Maybe only the Fourth Symphony passes a perfection-ist test. In *Das Lied von der Erde* the generally finely-woven tone and texture is brutally torn or bruised by the orchestral hurricane in the 'Trinklied vom Jammer der Erde', at the episode of the vision of the ape, after the words: 'Im Mondschein auf den Gräbern', etc. His use of banal tunes is justified by uncritical admirers of him for the reason that he is deliberately banal to emphasise ironic contrasts. The common, vulgar tune associated with the march of the world's rabble on the Day of Judge-ment, in the Second Symphony, is no doubt a stroke of ironic allusiveness. But there are times, many times, when the most devout of Mahlerians must feel uncomfortable if he happens to be listening to Mahler in the company of, say, a French musician brought up on Debussy, Fauré, Ravel, not to mention their classic forbears. Mahler asks for collabora-tion, not only from sensitive sympathetic ears. It is not too much to say that with Mahler, more than with any other composer, we need to be constantly on much the same psychological and temperamental wave-length as his sometimes oscillating own.

Our picture of him as man and composer will stand out in the boldest possible relief if we compare him with Richard Strauss. They were anti-podal: Strauss was everything that Mahler was not. Mahler was introvert, Strauss extrovert. Strauss's musical vision looked outward on the world, Mahler's turned inward. Though Mahler was a great conductor of opera, he could never have composed an opera. His imagination worked too egocentrically ever to project itself into other shapes or modes of con-sciousness. By no stretch of fancy can we think of Mahler's mind going into the world of the Marschallin, identifying itself with Sophie, Ochs, Oktavian. His music, non-erotic, has little wordly charm. He has no aristocratic reserves. He did not always remember his dignity—'Wahr' Er sein Dignité und fahr' Er ab.'[1] Strauss composed mostly with ease, always with facility. After he had received from Hofmannsthal the first scene of the first act of *Der Rosenkavalier* he wrote to him: 'Die Szene ist reizend, wird sich komponieren wie Öl und Butterschmalz.'[2] Composed itself! Not a note in all Mahler composed itself. He commanded a tech-nique and vocabulary of orchestral musical expression not less com-prehensive and masterful than Strauss's; but he could not use it just professionally or functionally, to perform a job of work. If his state of

[1] 'Remember your dignity and go!'
[2] 'The scene is charming and will compose itself and run as easily as butter or train-oil.'

mind and spirit were unresolved, disintegrated, unable to achieve unity, or in any condition of unrest or frustration, his music suffered the same way. 'One does not compose,' said Mahler. 'One is composed.' ('Man komponiert nicht, man wird komponiert.')

Mahler swore that he never wrote an insincere note. He, with all his immense orchestral culture and experienced skill, could not compose fluently. At the end of his life, as we have seen, some ease and mellowness entered his music, the ease and mellowness of a tired mind and soul, ready to depart. Strauss, I think, enjoyed his work more than any other composer, dead or alive; he knew that up his sleeve were all the aces. Mahler said that he and Strauss were tunnelling from different sides of the same mountain, and that one day they would meet. They will come together when, and not before, pleasurable indulgence lies down side by side with lean asceticism. For, if Mahler laughs and actually exults oftener than he is given credit for, it is because of a reaction, or a release, from a congenital and strained seriousness. He nursed a dæmon. Can we imagine a dæmonic Strauss, in whose company we could feel the presence of something inimical, unsocial, not at bottom approachable and amenable? Mahler is never *gemütlich*; even the songs of his early spring—*Lieder eines fahrenden Gesellen*—have a knife stabbing the breast. He did not compose to amuse the bourgeoisie. The fact that the Vienna Opera might be *ausverkauft* one night, not a seat vacant, was no consolation to him if the performance had not come up to his perfectionist ideal.

Yet for all his sincerity and integrity, for all his desperate striving to harmonise his spirit and to search out and dedicate himself to the beauty of the world, he cannot be called noble. He measures himself against Goethe and Dante; at any rate he did not hesitate to compose on their plane and conception. But he could not create a single tune or stretch of music which strikes us as noble. Every tone of Mahler is egocentric or redolent of some earthy material. He tends to weaken his line chromatically or go off at a tangent into some restless orchestral indulgence. If I may quote myself (and why not?) 'folksong in his music is answered by the romantic rhetoric of horn and brass. Into a tone-world of Styrian landscape and old village comes the languishing over-civilised string *portamento* of the city and concert hall, dripping with *Zärtlichkeit*.' In his setting of the second part of Goethe's *Faust* the *Mater Gloriosa* is invoked by a melody most lusciously appealing to the sensuous, impressionable ear:

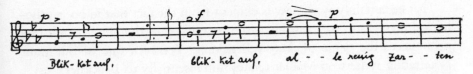

And when the *Mater Gloriosa* appears, harp and harmonium distil the essence of *Schmalz*, as I have already mentioned. The fact which is inexplicable to analysis is that Mahler in ignoble, or not exactly noble, musical language, can consummate his lofty intentions; we are persuaded by his persistent sincerity. It is the fervent, frequently exalted sound of his voice, not always what he says, that persuades us. I can well believe that non-Mahlerians find the flavour of *Schmalz* in the full-hearted melody of the invocation to beauty in the *Abschied* of *Das Lied*, where string *appoggiature* press out the juice. No austerity here; no instrumental self-denial. And there is no austerity at the end of the work, when celesta and mandoline enchant the ear with tintinnabulations that are far from world-renouncing.

V

At many a turn we run into the Mahler paradox. Though a Jew he wrote no Jewish music of traditional or synagogical accent. He has indeed been taken to task for not composing Hebraic music. Paul Rosenfeld, in his brilliant *Musical Portraits* (Kegan Paul, 1922), argued that, because Mahler lived in a society that made Judaism a curse, 'it was decreed that he suppressed in himself any strain or echo of the harsh accents of Hebrew music proper. Mahler would have been the first to have been repelled by the sound of his own harsh, haughty, guttural, abrupt Hebrew inflection . . . rather than speak his proper idiom he made, unaware to himself, perhaps, the choice of speaking through the voices of other men, of the great German composers.' I think this is a wrong-headed view, but it serves to consolidate mine: that Mahler composed no music in which a truly Hebraic voice is heard. He had to compose accordingly as environment and culture made him. His music, as a fact, has a cosmopolitanism which we associate with the Jew who has assimilated a culture from the environment into which the wanderings of his race have tossed him, or his stock. It was scarcely a limitation in him that he transcended racial exclusiveness. That he was a Jew who composed like an Austrian of his period is not an unnatural phenomenon. But it all adds to the Mahler complex contributing to our study of his music.

That he certainly was a Jew is evident from the fact that in no psychological or stylistic way can his name be spoken in the same breath that pronounces the name of Anton Bruckner. Yet even one of our most penetrating writers on Mahler relates him essentially to Bruckner:

'They [Bruckner and Mahler] were, in fact, attached to each other by mutual friendship and high esteem, despite their disparity of age,' maintains Dr. H. F. Redlich (*Bruckner and Mahler:* J. M. Dent, Master Musicians Series). 'The works by which they will be remembered first and foremost were written, planned or completed in the Austrian capital. Both were deeply imbued with the spiritual heritage of the Roman Church. Their music is permeated by folkloristic elements of old Austria. . . .'

Omnipotence itself could not without unusual labour produce two natures, two temperaments, more different and contrary than Bruckner's and Mahler's. Bruckner's tone, diction and symphonic structure are characteristics of an integrated man: the sturdy terraced orchestration, the consistent *tempi*. When Bruckner has stated a measured period he takes a patient breath and then resumes his confident way. Mahler called Bruckner half god, half simpleton, neither of which terms could he apply to himself. Bruckner's solidly-scored, organ-toned orchestra, his embracing rhythm, his confidence that bars and bars of reiterated fanfares will bring him safely to the journey's end—here are the marks of a mind and spirit sure of faith, dedicated to 'der liebe Gott'. Mahler's faith, not as steadfast or definable as Bruckner's, was one symptom among others of his search for anchorage in a world in which he ran down corridor after corridor seeking he knew not what. The nervous tensions to be felt in Mahler's music nearly everywhere are entirely absent from Bruckner's. Consider only a Scherzo of Bruckner, and one of Mahler. Geniality and peasant sanity in broad rustic play, God-in-nature: such is the theme and atmosphere of a Bruckner Scherzo. But the Mahler Scherzo is ironic, angular, nocturnal, spectral; the rhythm and orchestral colours are complex, not simple. Mahler emulated Bruckner's evocations of the chorale, but usually for dramatic effect. For example, the chorale interlude in the development of the first movement of the Seventh Symphony of Mahler enters as a mysterious nature tone. The Mahler birdcalls and distant fanfares are eerie sounds in a dark bodeful region. Bruckner's chorales are always symbols of his faith; never does he call on them as dramatic protagonists. Bruckner's great octave unisons are reliant, spacious as the mountain's ranging undulations. The texture of a Mahler symphony is, nine bars out of ten, nervously contrapuntal, with parts tensely individual, unready to mingle in easeful harmony. I would no more relate Mahler to Bruckner, in mind, temperament and musical speech than I would relate Edgar Allen Poe to Wordsworth. It is agreed by all who know what they are talking about that Hofmannesque visitations flicker over the Mahler scene from time to time, evidence enough of how far removed Mahler was from the sane, four-square world of Bruckner. In the Scherzo of his Ninth Symphony Bruckner, admittedly, leaves the bluff peasant air and goes into an elfin or gnomic subterrannean region; but there is no nervous debility in this original movement in which Bottom galumphs and Ariel dances on fantastic toe. If it is true, as Redlich says, that one of the essential features of Bruckner's first movements is their primordial character and gradual emergence from the sonorus nebulae of fundamental harmony, Bruckner is in command, announcing a *Fiat Lux*. He was not a sophisticated composer, unlike Mahler again. But he was the greater man, because he was the more resolved in his elements, loftier of thought and consequently less egocentric. He had no vanity; he was, as I say, God-intoxicated. Mahler was tormented by a perpetual persistent *Ich*. 'My symphonies', he said, 'exhaust the content of my entire existence. Whoever listens to my music intelligently will see my life transparently revealed.' He could have summed-up his musical life and all his works in the words of Goethe's *Tasso*:

> Nein, alles ist dahin! Nur eines bleibt:
> Die Träne hat uns die Natur verliehen,
> Den Schrei des Schmerzens, wenn der Mann zuletzt
> Es nicht mehr erträgt. Und mir noch über alles—
> Sie liess im Schmerz mir Melodie und Rede,
> Die tiefste Fülle meiner Not zu klagen:
> Und wenn der Mensch in seiner Qual verstummt,
> Gab mir ein Gott, zu sagen wie ich leide.[1]

[1] *Torquato Tasso* by Goethe: 'Now all is finished. Nothing left now, only the tears given us by nature, and the cry from the heart when man can no longer endure his pain. To me, above all, she gave melody and words, so that I could sing of my deepest sorrow. Others may be dumb in their sufferings but God gave me a gift to tell of mine.'

When this likening of Mahler to Goethe's *Tasso* was written I had no idea that the same parallel had occurred to Bruno Walter (*Gustav Mahler*, Hamish Hamilton).

The music of Mahler is permeated by symbols conveying broadly the emotional and mental states in which Mahler found himself as he composed. We must listen to him first with the musical ear; on this point I am obliged to insist more and more as we, you who are reading and I who am writing, are drawn into the Mahler psychology and argument. On his own admission Mahler needed words as a sort of blue-print from which his musical art could begin. And as he wrote songs and quoted from them in his symphonies, either literally or by implication, we can easily find in his music in bulk certain themes and instrumental groupings and colourings which by association with a poetic text, give us clues to what he is in varying ways saying, even where he has dispensed with verbal clues. For example, in his First Symphony during the ironic funeral-march third movement, Mahler modulates to G major and remembers a nostalgic phrase in the fourth song of the *Lieder eines fahrenden Gesellen* cycle, where the linden tree stands under whose blossoms the love-jilted swain has found rest. We begin to learn this way the associative values of Mahler's basic tone material. They are as identifiable as any Wagner *leit-motif*. The most recurrent theme in Mahler clearly denotes his state of lost-ness in the world. It emerges for the first time unmistakably in the third movement of the Fourth Symphony. It is a theme which moves upward, beginning with the intervals of a third, major or minor, urging itself rather than rising freely, with an ache which can be felt. Many times an *appoggiatura* wrings out the note of longing:

A

We get a hint of this entirely *Mahlerisch* motif as early as the First Symphony, in the middle section of the Finale: the *sehr gesangvoll* melody:

B

The remarkable fact about this motif is that during the two years separat-

ing the completion of the Fourth and the beginning of the Fifth Symphonies, Mahler, now setting Rückert's poem 'Ich bin der Welt abhanden
gekommen', began this way:

C1

And again he revealed his hand and heart in the phrase

C2

As late as *Das Lied von der Erde* this melody of identity clings to Mahler
in various guises; where he (or the singer) waits in a vacant twilight for
sign of a friend:

D

It follows him spectrally to the end—in the Adagio of the Ninth Symphony:

E

We should know, then, who is talking to us and what he is saying in the
Adagietto of the Fifth Symphony:

F

In the beautifully reposeful beginning of the Adante of the Sixth Symphony comes the old refrain—'die alte Weise':

G

I know of no other instance in symphonic (or any other) music where
throughout a composer's corpus a single personally-flavoured motif is
constantly coming in, a distant voice which reveals the same psychology
no matter how much it is varied in key, instrumental colour or harmony.
I have found numerous points in the scores at which a modulation can be
made admitting entrance to the theme—points where Mahler himself has
not used it. But it is implied, omnipresent. The reader who has a gift for
instrumental modulation might amuse and instruct himself by attempting
a natural transition to the motif after the cadence of the ninth bar of the
Adagio of the Ninth Symphony; or after the fourth bar of the first vocal
phrase in 'Der Einsame im Herbst' of *Das Lied von der Erde*. Try the
modulation from the A flat.

In a period of composition when German and Austrian music wallowed
in succulent harmony from which melody was often only an extension or
variation of the basic chords, Mahler concentrated on independence of
parts. It is advisable to make this point again and again in this discussion
of Mahler—even at the risk of repetition—for only by some such insistence will the legend of his essential musical softness be dispersed.
Dr Redlich has stated the truth about Mahler as harmonist, stated it
in language so beautifully precise that I am not vain enough to try to
improve on it:

'It is characteristic of him to think of music, generally speaking, in
terms of thematic antithesis rather than as melody supported by an
undercurrent of ever changing harmony.'

Starkly uncompromising antithesis at that! Even at the moment of
titillation of the ears he also addresses our appreciation of freely-moving
part writing:

Poco adagio (**Fourth Symphony: third movement**)

As familiar as any 'look' of a page of a Mahler score is this, from the first movement of the Ninth Symphony:

'People who say Mahler is "familiar",' said a member of the Wiener Philharmoniker to me one day, 'and made up of the stock orchestral clichés, should come and try to play him.'

Mahler's use of bare intervals (as Dr Redlich has pointed out and as anybody else who will take the trouble to examine a Mahler score will see) eventually leads to an emancipation of the fourth and fifth, paving the way for a concept of music almost based on combinations of these two intervals and to a codification of their possibilities. A forgotten critic accused Mahler of being unable to compose substantial bass parts, having no doubt been led astray by the scarcity in Mahler, compared with symphonists in general of his day, of rooted primary harmony. His adaptation of a free counterpoint to a 'romantic' or expressive purpose was one of his contributions to formal expansion of the symphony; and in this, of course, he was preceded by Berlioz. But Berlioz—this will surprise you—was not, as a shaper of music, as classically bred as Mahler.

Another prevalent figure or motif in Mahler is one of short notes often *pizzicato*, throbbing and trembling or stabbing in isolation, after a climax or as a transition passage to a relaxed mood, even if a melancholy one. We hear it in the early *Gesellen* cycle, before the 'Leise, bis zum Schluss', section beginning 'By the wayside stood a linden tree':

We hear it after the first climax in the slow movement of the Fourth Symphony, in the harp:

This is no merely conventional piece of padding; no case of a composer just marking time, as we shall hear at the crisis of the first movement of the Ninth Symphony, during the apocalyptic funeral march ('Wie ein Kondukt'):

It is a cue for a psychological as well as a tonal change. It is an omniscient protagonist in *Das Lied von der Erde*:

The Mahler scores are a breeding-ground of expression marks which anticipate every orchestral emergency or tonal need. Only *Rauchen verboten* is omitted. We can well believe from the evidence of them that, as conductor, Mahler did not let the music speak for itself: he does not let his own music do that. He is, so to say, for ever drawing our attention. He is constantly using musical italic:

Really he was a composer with an inferiority complex. If he can give us a theme of large span, twenty bars and more of a curve, we may be sure that in its flight of movement there are pulsations or tensions of strain or doubt by the way. In all Mahler there is not a single sturdy scale passage such as strides sturdily up and down a Bruckner movement.

Mahler has for half a century been accused of orchestral bombast, of orchestral elephantiasis, of a reckless piling of instrumental Pelian on Ossa. And circumstantial evidence admittedly can be got together making a plausible case for the prosecution, despite his quite aggressive insistence on counterpoint, his often angular line. A single glance at the scores of the Fifth, Sixth and Seventh Symphonies, or at the inner movements of the Ninth, shows music as if under an X-ray, bones and criss-cross nerves, contrasting strongly with the well-fleshed harmonic coverings revealed by a Brahms score. But in the same symphonies, in the slow or slower movements, you will find strings yearning with nuance, the composer's expression marks almost hectically numerous. The violins stretch to heights and the basses grope in depths, while wood-wind play plaintively in between. Always the Mahler ambivalence as in the life of the man himself. Problem child and at the same time a musical thinker and an orchestral magician! He can be so restrained of tone that some-times a vast Mahler canvas seems suddenly vacant, untenanted except for a few instruments seeking to find a tonal centre. Then pandemonium breaks out in brass and timpani; the entire tonal structure collapses, as at the end of the first movement of the Second Symphony. Yet Mahler's sonorities are seldom weighty or colossal because of thick blocks of harmony. The tumult is one of contending parts or of rhythms suddenly entangled.

When all is said and done, when all the Mahler storms have come and gone, we are compelled time after time to stress the fact that the main feature is the clearness and exposed identity of the scoring. Mahler was the first symphonic composer to make nearly every instrument a protagonist speaking in its own voice. Berlioz pointed the way to this kind of individualisation; Mahler coming later, and as a conductor in a position to learn every trick of the trade up to the latest moment, was able to enlarge his tonal encyclopedia and more and more give the significance he needed to his instrumental dramatis personae. Take, for example, the sound of the horn as it intones in the Scherzo of the Fifth Symphony in a sudden silence:

M

The horn here has a colour and suggestiveness hard to define, but it certainly is not the comfortably romantic horn known in Mahler's day. This is at one and the same time a horn seductive to the senses yet inimical. At the opposite extreme is the jubilant transformation-scene use of the horn in the Fourth Symphony, opening the gates of the children's paradise.

Mahler, the spectacular romantic, a singer of dying falls; as we have seen—more than once in this book—Mahler at times answers to this description. But he built, once he had found himself, from classic foundations. His conceptions were romantic and, for all his wordy theories to the contrary, programmatic, or half-programmatic. But in his structure he used the traditional symphonic forms often enough, if not always. The Fifth and Seventh Symphonies each end in an elaborate Rondo. Mahler could put on an unmistakably academic cloak. The part-writing of the Fifth Symphony is masterfully and dutifully classic. The first part of the Eighth is a *tour de force* of sonata form. Sonata form is common enough in Mahler, serving as a blue-print; but the edifice eventually put up has a more than classical interior decoration. The first movement of the Third Symphony and the Finale of the Sixth have two development sections each. There are four movements to the First, five to the Fifth, four in the Sixth, five in the Seventh, two in the Eighth, six in *Das Lied von der Erde*, and four in the Ninth.

So there we are: a composer who draws us to him with one hand and thrusts us away with the other. A genius; potentially one of the most powerful and original known to music. With a technique considerably in advance in its resources, and the way he applied it, of any other composer of his period, he shaped his world—a world of will and representation. 'Eine Symphonie schaffen, heisst mir', was his creed, 'mit allen Mitteln der vorhandenen Technik mir eine Welt aufbauen'. From all the technique at hand he would build his world, with himself the only inhabitant. Schönberg wrote to Mahler after hearing one of his symphonies: 'I saw the forces of evil and good wrestling with each other. I saw a man struggling towards inward harmony. I divined a personality, a drama, and truthfulness, the most uncompromising truthfulness.' True: Mahler never wrote an insincere note. The symphonies were his world; it is time we went into them in some detail and sequence.

THE SYMPHONIES

Symphony No. 1 in D Major

FOUR MOVEMENTS

1884–88

THE FIRST FOUR symphonies, sometimes called the *Wunderhorn* group, are related one to another by quotations from songs composed in his early twenties, some of them set to verses selected from the famous collection of German folklore called *Des Knaben Wunderhorn*. But before Mahler chanced to come across this anthology he had composed his song-cycle, *Lieder eines fahrenden Gesellen*, to his own words, which are so much akin in spirit and atmosphere to the anthology that by the miraculous intuition of genius Mahler had, so to say, been talking *Wunderhorn* prose for years without knowing it.

But the influence of Mahler's *Wunderhorn* quotations on his symphonies has been greatly exaggerated. They had no influence more obtrusive than the *Wesendonck* songs in the capacious texture of *Tristan und Isolde*. The *Lied* in a Mahler symphony is not a germ or seed of 'folky' or regional music. Mahler the Jew felt none of the 'nationalistic' urges stirring among composers round about 1880. Mahler had no time for local colour as such. The lilting tune of the second of the *Lieder eines fahrenden Gesellen* ('Songs of a Travelling Journeyman' is the comically inadequate English translation) trips into the incalculable region of the First Symphony unaware that soon it will be caught up in a tone-world already *Mahlerisch* in profusion of ironic contrasts. The *Lied* in Mahler can be taken as symbol of the nature-loving, the trustful adolescent side of his character. But it is not a musical *idée fixe*, a melody representative of an Austro-Jewish Harold in Moravia. Mahler's quotations from himself are used, whatever extra-musical hints they may convey, as strictly symphonically as Beethoven uses the theme that opens the *Eroica*.

More significantly illuminating for Mahler's creative future than the *Wunderhorn* songs is the youthful *Das klagende Lied*, composed when Mahler was not more than nineteen. This *Lied* tells us of two brothers, both in love with the same princess. One murders the other and conceals

the body deep in a wood. A wandering minstrel finds a bone, carves it
into a flute or pipe, and when he plays on it the grisly secret is revealed.
This 'prentice work sniffs the Mahler dark, tragic tone-colour far ahead;
the music is already, as Donald Mitchell has searched out, dislocating
abruptly, the texture steely and inimical. The work is poignantly prophetic. Music was for Mahler often (but, remember, not always!) a *klagendes
Lied*. The instruments he played upon were always revealing to him
buried bones.

First Movement

The First Symphony, completed in 1888, on the surface of its structure
is not violently progressive beyond its period. Seven horns merely shared
or extended the practice of Richard Strauss, whose *Don Juan* was a
product of much the same period. The symphony's form is after the four-
movement tradition, and Mahler's unification of his first ambitious work
by a reviewing of themes in the Finale was, no doubt, homage to
Beethoven.

But the young composer carried to unprecedented lengths the integration of all four movements by thematic and rhythmic transformation.
Maybe the themes and rhythms are in themselves not always impressive.
Sometimes I fancy Mahler was less interested in a theme for its own
musical appeal than for its ability, at a psychological prompting, to
change and yet remain the same thing. The introduction to the first
movement evokes a vision of the Austrian landscape at dawn with a
tone—a *Lokalton*—never before heard in symphonic music:

1

The preliminary bars, obvious 'tone painting', were all too likely in 1889
to make audiences suspicious of yet another of the 'impure' symphonic

poems then popular with composers. Mahler sinned even more palpably against the classical habit by adapting the poetically descending fourth to a cuckoo call:

Moreover, in its context it sounds unmistakably like a cuckoo-call; yet from time immemorial the call had been musically represented by the interval of a third. Mahler uses the motif not entirely as a means of pictorial suggestiveness, but as a composer making a consequential symphony. This interval of the fourth is the main germ-cell from which the entire work evolves. For example: in the Finale the triumphant bell-ringing apotheosis is based on:

in which the interval of the fourth, in the first place a mysterious nature-tone, is surprisingly and even blatantly 'translated'. The symphony might well be called the 'apotheosis of the fourth'. Into the first movement, after the landscape and its horizon have been unfolded, with distant calls from the barracks mingling with the cuckoo's, a melody taken from the second of the *Lieder eines fahrenden Gesellen* comes in easefully:

Again the interval of the fourth. And the second movement, in *Waltz-Ländler* form, begins with a stamping figure in the bass; also the fourth:

The Waltz is set into motion this way.

6

The third, fourth and fifth bars reproduce in cunning guise the same notes of the beginning of the *Gesell'* song. Here is a metamorphosis of notation which so easily deceives the ear (if not the eye) that it is a reasonable supposition that the composer himself has not been conscious of it. But Mahler throughout this 'prentice symphony achieves a remarkably surprising and apt plasticity.

While the bugles and cuckoos are echoing in the prelude, a chromatic figure crawls up from the depths of the 'cellos and basses:

7

The triplet, here surreptitious and hidden, becomes a snarling protagonist in the Finale:

8

It has sometimes been my fancy that this chromatic motif was conceived, perhaps subconsciously from the old *Frère Jacques* cannon on which the slow movement is based:

9

Mahler's way of ringing the changes on his themes is not characteristic of a naïve composer. He has constantly been described as naïve, presumably because of his preoccupation in his less mature works with the *Wunderhorn* folk-lore. A naïve Jew is a complex scarcely in nature. Mahler, from early manhood onward, reveals in his music the sharpness of intellect and the cosmopolitan sophistications of a man whose genius was constantly nervous with the restless temperament and curiosity of his race in our times.

After the *Gesell'* song has entered the movement and lilted its way with many happy touches and turns, such as:[1]

10

the D major brightness fades. The fundamental tone deepens; and in the 'cellos we hear mournful, even menacing, *glissandi*:

11

which develop into:

12

and the *glissando* figure is then rather astonishingly absorbed into a lyrically warm extension of the main theme (when we reach the development proper).

[1] Mahler uses a repeat sign at the end of this *Gesell'* section—a young man's obeisance to classic symphonic usage. But he really had no time for internal repetitions. Only once again, in the Sixth Symphony does he use a repeat sign. I think conductors should ignore the repeat in this most original 'prentice work.

13

It is the same two-note descending slide which serves as the bodeful pendulum swinging the first movement's climax and forcing home the symphony's Finale:

14

The metamorphoses of themes in this symphony, indeed, not only of musical interest but significant of psychological or dramatic variations, are such that to dissect them in the familiar analytical terms ('the harp takes over the theme, once again in D major over a pedal A') would be as illuminating as if a dramatic critic, discussing say, *Timon of Athens*, wrote: 'Re-enter Timon and Flavius' and left it at that, without telling us something of what they are talking about.

I have said that themes in a Mahler symphony—especially this First— are a sort of dramatis personae. It is no use at all listening to them as first and second subjects, and so on. The beginning of what might be regarded as the formal development—though Mahler is at his protean exercises from the first bar—is announced by a very definite musical (or orchestral entity) though like others it is compact of the fourth:

15

Technically this assertive horn tune ends as well as begins the development; but really it serves as an important resolving protagonist, as sort of decisive 'messenger'. In the course of the development the second theme or subject (Ex. 13) an extension of the *Gesell'* motif, merges into:

16

and

17

As Dr Erwin Stein pointed out, Mahler was the first composer to carry on themes from an exposition to a development section. Another derivation from the introduction's stealthy chromatic figure, (Ex. 15) is the womb from which springs, in the Finale, the first confident summons to decisive and, in the fashion of the period, rhetorical symphonic resolution.

The crisis of the first movement, leading to the recapitulation, is a tremendous pendulum motion, culminating in the introduction's bugle calls, heaved along by a sublime chromatic pull in the brass and woodwind. The recapitulation itself is given over to the *Gesell'* theme and its immediately recognisable offspring; the exposition is telescoped. At the end, in violent reiterations of the cuckoo call, the bird is decisively silenced, if not strangled.

Second Movement

The second movement, in *Waltz-Ländler* form, begins, as we have already noted, with a stamping figure of the interval of the fourth in the bass:

18

And the Waltz is set into motion this way:

19

The third, fourth and fifth bars of this quotation, reproducing in different guises the same tones which begin the *Gesell'* theme, is a kind of metamorphosis which marks Mahler off starkly from Bruckner, whose *scherzi* are naïve in their direct and manly open-air rhythms. Mahler developed the *scherzo* in time to evoke a world of shadowy, veiled romantic atmosphere and action; in this, his first, though he starts from a bucolic stamping dance, soon the country air is flavoured by the whiff of *Schmalz* and the town-bred Viennese Waltz:

20

and

21

We are here not far from the environment of vinous-breathed Baron Ochs. Yet the material, familiar and worldly in a way which could not possibly have emanated from the 'pure' mind of Bruckner, is treated by the most civilised art, with transitions of tone and *tempo* quite out of the common symphonic usage of more than half a century ago. A bare schematic analysis of the Scherzo reveals the working-out of five motives, the bass stamping interval of the fourth more or less persistent, except in the Trio; and the recapitulation is a concentration of the movement's first part.

It is a movement which is not certain to be respectably regarded by one and all, despite the formal adherence to the classical A-B-A sections. The content, as we have seen, is 'popular', at times bordering on *Kitsch*.

It has none of the sublimity which we feel in a Beethoven *scherzo*, even the most unbuttoned of them. It has none of the square rotundity or the bourgeois amiability of a Brahms or a Schumann *scherzo*. It has rhythmical wildness and uncouthness; and also it gives us a familiar *Ländler* melody, not 'natural' but 'garnished'. The technique, the orchestration and dynamics, are in advance of its period's usage in German or Austrian music. Its hard percussiveness, combined with the abandoned nervous tonal excesses of horns and trumpets, foretell the breathless instrumental somersaultings of the *Rondo Burleske* of the Ninth Symphony. There is less of melodic or rhythmical invention in the *Scherzo* than an invention of dynamic contrast, and an accumulation of pounding stamping or- chestral mass, with daring bravura of instrumental parts. The movement, a bastard of classical minuet origin, is really an interlude, preparatory to the symphony's progress to a psychological denouement. We have now left the *Gesell'* and the friendly landscape and *Wirtshaus* behind; in the third and fourth movements, Mahler turns his vision inward and finds ironic questionings and grimaces before he hammers them out. Not until we come to a flash-back in the finale do we hear again the cuckoo's fourth again, or the lilt of the *Gesell'* song. The chromatic motif takes charge in the next movement as the villain of the piece: a smiling villain, sometimes.

THIRD MOVEMENT

One of Mahler's most remarkable gifts enabled him to take a common- place or familiar-sounding theme and give it a curious twist or treatment so that it served his musico-psychological purpose. It is because of this aptitude to transform a naïve melody or rhythm that he has been thought of as a naïve composer by critics who have apparently not looked deeply into the scores. The third movement is based on the old tune of *Frère Jacques*; I remember having it sung to me in my childhood, though how it had journeyed over the centuries to a grimy suburb of Manchester I cannot tell. It goes like this:

The movement begins with a muffled drum, *pp*:

23

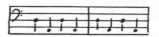

Again the fourth—and bless thee, how thou art translated! No longer the daylight of D major. The movement is obviously a mock funeral-march; as such, at any rate, it fascinated me when I heard it for the first time. I was then delighted to find out that Mahler was originally inspired to it by a drawing of the French engraver Jacques Callot, depicting a funeral procession of animals carrying the corpse (in a coffin) of the hunter. This picture is one of my most engaging possessions. The coffin is carried by stags and a fox sits on top of the coffin, a boar is the gravedigger. The hares are waving flags, and there is a band of musicians—cats, frogs, crows— while birds fly above, everybody obviously celebrating an occasion. In a performance conducted by Mitropolous the movement was given just the right snap to fit in with Callot's quaint irony. But Mahler later clouded the picture by declaring:

'It is quite irrelevant to know what is being described—it is important only to grasp the mood which is being expressed, and from which the fourth movement springs like a flash of lightning from a sombre cloud. It is simply the cry of a deeply wounded heart which is preceded by the close atmosphere of the funeral march. . . .'

We needn't, of course, as we listen to the movement, think of animals bearing a huntsman to a well-deserved grave; though our enjoyment of it will not suffer if we do, for clearly Callot's engraving prompted the music's parodying illustrative touches. The animals are unmistakably smirking and quirking with glee in this phrase:

24

With the Callot fantasy in our mind we are not far from the psychological clue. Mahler's love of animals and all nature was of the sort that would

have sadistically exulted over a Huntsman's Funeral in real life and see in
it an ironical symbol of justice being done. Our appreciation of Mahler's
bitter-sweet brand of humour is quickened if we make some imaginative
allusiveness to the Callot engraving. On the other hand, if we listen to the
movement too seriously, contemplating wounded hearts and all the rest,
it is possible that we might think that the music is not sufficiently tragic
in gait to warrant Mahler's revised and more solemn description of its
place in the scheme. The onslaught of the Finale is not weakened if we
think so—and find the atmosphere of the funeral march too close and
conventionally funerary (which the music really isn't). On the contrary,
as we relish the burlesque of the animals' cortège, we are, by the contrast
of satirical and rhetorical moods and temper, all the readier to sympathise
with young Mahler's efforts to tear passion to rags and storm the heavens
with an apotheosis-finale such as even Beethoven would not wish to scale.

The march counter-theme is the first of the naughty grimaces, from the
oboe:

25

Pizzicato, cymbals and big drum take part in the grotesquerie; and the
high born classically-bred symphonic traditionalists of the 1880s had good
cause to be scandalised by the fingers-to-the-nose snap of

25A

Two E-flat clarinets, bassoon, bass tuba, flutes, trumpets clearly character-
ise a profane jubilation to an *oomp-a* accompaniment. The music can also
be taken as a sign of Mahler's Mephistophelian contempt for the bestiality
of life. But the sarcasm melts in the first of many *Mahlerisch* transitions,
on a low earth-tone, above which the harp in syncopations evokes the
soon-to-be-familiar *Mahlerisch* hesitations as the air clears. (See the
characteristic examples Exs. H and I, p. 30.)

From the muted violins emerges:

Once more the fourth. But the melody is another quotation from the *Lieder eines fahrenden Gesellen*, the fourth of the cycle where the melancholy lover says farewell and sees a vision of the linden tree and finds rest. The song is marvellously woven into the movement's tissue, so much so that we are left wondering if it emerged again from Mahler's subconsciousness as he was composing his First Symphony. This reposeful section of the funeral march is entirely related, by the mysterious processes of imaginative metamorphosis, to the preceding section, different though the two tone-worlds may be, the one rude and satirical, the other idyllic. The reappearance of the interval of the fourth in this case must, I think, be regarded as not designed, though other commentators, notably German, have decided that here is yet another example of Mahler's thematic aptness. As I have said, I take a delight in supposing that the chromatic figure which steals into the introduction of the first movement (Ex. 7), is a sort of prophecy of the beginning of the funeral march. The return to the march does not lead to an exact formal recapitulation. The parody feeds on itself; the pace of the cortège quickens, with impudent jerked accents, as though in a profane hurry to deposit the corpse where no more harm can be done:

Then gradually, through changes of key and, more potent, changes of instrumental colour and gait, the movement descends to a twilit orchestral graveyard, the interval of the fourth beating the mock mourner's tread. Softer and softer fall the padded notes in the darkening orchestra —in the growing silence the main funeral theme persists, with echoes from the *Gesell'* song 'Lieb' und Leid und Welt und Traum'. Then the fourth movement follows without a pause.

FOURTH MOVEMENT

Pandemonium, a dissonant chord (C, F, A flat, B, D flat) screaming in the wind; and an up-and-down rush of strings, with a signal:

28

and a chromatic snarl:

29

The triplet, born of the passive but potentially chromatic visitant to the symphony's introduction, has become a violent and actual protagonist. For nearly fifty bars it contends against the headlong race of the strings and the efforts of the signal to assert itself. The convulsion subsides. Now the main theme of the movement marches in:

I quote this theme in full for two reasons. It is a typical Mahler quick tune, an angular sort of march, with a 'tic'. (Mahler himself walked in a

D

jerky way.) Such a theme is constantly recurring in a quick Mahler movement; he never marches on broad confidently striding phrases.

Also the theme, though on the face of it commonplace and unsymphonic, is really far from sterile. The phrase marked A refers back to Ex. 17 of the first movement. And the phrase marked B is cunningly adapted from Ex. 13, the extension of the *Gesell'* song of the first movement. Moreover, the first five bars are the fulcrum of the symphony's triumphant apotheosis. The theme has absorbed the triplet figure for a moment. And the downward leaps are the pendulum which germinated in the *glissandi* of Ex. 11.

So lengthy a motif calls for bifurcation; and Mahler artfully rings the changes on phrase A as well as on phrase B. As a fact, Mahler in his First Symphony's Finale is adapting and reviewing basic material in a lengthy exposition some hundred-and-seventy bars long. The chromatic figure and the signal fight it out in a kind of academic contention of violin semiquavers and rising brass announcements of the first four notes of the movement's opening theme (Ex. 30). The notes (too many!) exhaust themselves in a '*mit grosser Wildheit*' whirlwind, which ends in a shudder of strings and in the distance a muted echo of the chromatic triplet figure. Then Mahler gives us one of his most characteristically alluring modulations, as the strings yearn upwards:

31

followed by a long-phrased forty-six-bar melody, beautifully flavoured with the Mahler *Schmalz*:

31A

The chromatic triplet, even, has been drawn into the general allurement. And a horn cadence is memorable:

32

This song of uninhibited sentiment is, I suppose, technically the movement's second subject. As it swoons away in aromatic pain, the chromatic theme comes stealing in again (first heard in the symphony's introduction). The chromatic triplet snarls once more, and the trumpets sound the signal for the battle of the development, which is worked out with that curious stiff almost pedantic emphasis which occasionally came upon the least pedantic of all composers since Beethoven. The signal theme wins through to:

33

In the development some ingenious play is made of a phrase from the long-drawn-out melody of *Schmalzig* contentment:

34

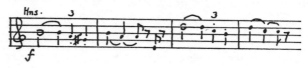

Frankly, this is a sticky moment; and the movement's goal seems to be becoming, quite donnishly, a peroration, with

35

The symphony's embryonic fourth has assumed a ringing if conventionally culminating stature. But Mahler springs a surprise in a supremely imaginative flash-back to the work's beginning: the nature tune in D minor, cuckoo calls, the rising chromatic intrusion, bugle calls, all dissolving into truly poetic fantasy, as the oboe sings the *Schmalz* song, and the strings wring the last juice out of it:

36

A snap of another chromatic, fresh to the fray, breaks the spell:

The recapitulation first treats the movement's main germ theme in a rather stiff, quasi-fugal way, which spins into another variant of the first movement's *Gesell'* continuation melody (Ex. 13) and from the descending leap of notes we are swung by the pendulum of the first movement again; and at its crisis in a fanfare of intensely energetic jubilation the symphony clinchingly sounds the triumphant apotheosis:

38

in which the fairly fruitful interval of the fourth has the last word or chime, which goes on rather too long. Mahler, as we shall often need to remark, never could make an end without emphasis. But when this First Symphony does finish the two crotchets snap out a dismissal of us as peremptory as any of Sibelius's.

This last movement really sounds much more skilfully composed than might be gathered on a first hearing. (My own reaction at my first performance was much the same as that of *The Times* critic, who thought it consisted mainly of 'balderdash'.) The play and counterplay of the themes, new and recalled, is extremely sharp-minded. As a young man's work it is astonishingly masterful and original in its plastic power, its perpetually inventive energy in development and adaptation, whatever the themes themselves may present to us of enduring musical value. The flavour of Mahler is in every bar; it is the most original symphony, I think, of the nineteenth century.

At its first performance in Pest the work was received with ribald laughter. Mahler himself said that nobody understood his language, pointing out at the same time that communication between composer and listener depended on certain accepted conventions or symbols, current expressive coin, so to say. Haydn prepared the ear for Beethoven, Weber for Wagner, and so on. 'They have no idea,' he complained, meaning the public, 'of what I am saying. My music is senseless and incomprehensible to them.' Ironically, in our own time Mahler has been charged with plagiarism, right and left. His First Symphony still shocks the 'classic' symphonic susceptibilities. First, because it suggests here and there a descriptive programme. Mahler originally called the symphony a symphonic-poem in two parts, with highly romantic titles for the movements: 'Days of Youth'; 'Commedia Umana'; 'Dall' inferno al Paradiso'. At the end of his life he described one of the *scherzi* of the unfinished Tenth Symphony 'Purgatorio' (or Inferno). He further put audiences off the track of his First by calling it 'Titan'—which naturally brought up expectations of Olympic grandeur. A less Greek mind and nature than Mahler's would be beyond the creative capacity of omnipotence. 'Titan' really belonged to a novel of period sentiment and grotesquerie by Jean Paul.

We can easily imagine what the musical taste of 1888, a taste accustomed to a certain symphonic consistency of diction, made of the First Symphony. I cannot agree with the admirable Dr H. F. Redlich that the *Frère Jacques* movement 'clearly derives' at any part from the second subject of the Finale of Schubert's C major. If Mahler had taken the first melody of the 'Unfinished' and merely scored it the change would have been from a purity to a certain impurity of musical diction. No matter how 'popular' Schubert occasionally sounds he is never assertive, self-consciously parodying or banal. But, as I say, this unique First Symphony at its worst is not as bad as it sounds. At its best—the first movement's introduction and the flash-back of the Finale—it is a sure hint of the originality and power to come, in intermittent but fascinating flashes, and sometimes long illuminations of genius.

Symphony No. 2 in C minor

FIVE MOVEMENTS

with soprano, contralto and chorus

(1887-94)

WITH THE Second Symphony we arrive at the *Wunderhorn* trilogy so called because in this, the Third and the Fourth, Mahler called on poems from the anthology already set to music by him. The *Wunderhorn* poetry nourished his mind and nature in so far as it elucidated his religious and pantheistic feelings about life and the world, here and hereafter, feelings in which an all-embracing love, making all creation kin, was the main factor. He later became a Catholic, mainly for reasons of expediency in a Vienna sulphurously anti-Semitic. As Dr Redlich, wittily quoting Heine, put it: 'Baptism was for him what it had been seventy-odd years earlier for Heine—"the admission to European culture".'

But the Second Symphony is not truly *Wunderhorn* in style, diction or expressive purpose. It reaches beyond the *Wunderhorn* fancies and conceits; it is prophetic of the Eighth Symphony in sweep of instrumental and choral canvas, and in its maturity of ethical and mystical vision. Mahler published a 'programme' descriptive of its 'meaning', then withdrew it out of fear that he would confuse the musical and symphonic issue. Here it is:

First Movement

We are standing beside the coffin of a man beloved. For the last time in his life, his battles, his sufferings and his purpose pass before the mind's eye. And now, at this deeply stirring moment, when we are released from the paltry distractions of everyday life, our hearts are gripped by a voice of awe-inspiring solemnity, which we seldom or never hear above the deafening traffic of mundane affairs. What next? it says. What is life?—and what is death? Have we any continued existence? Is it all an empty dream or has this life of ours, and after death, a meaning? If we are to go on living, we must answer this question.

The next three movements are conceived as intermezzo.

Second Movement: Andante

A blissful moment in his [the departed's] life; and a mournful memory of youth and lost innocence.

Third Movement: Scherzo

The spirit of unbelief and negation has taken possession of him. Looking into the turmoil of appearance, he loses together with the clear eyes of childhood the sure foothold which love alone gives. He despairs of himself and of God. The world and life become a witch's brew; disgust of existence in every form strikes him with iron fist and drives him to an outburst of despair.

Fourth Movement: The Primal Dawn (Alto Solo)

The mourning voice of ingenuous belief sounds in our ears. 'I am from God and will return to God! God will give me a candle to light me to the bliss of eternal life.'

Fifth Movement

We are confronted once more by terrifying questions. A voice is heard crying aloud. The end of all living things is come; the Last Judgement is at hand and the horror of the Day of days has come. The earth quakes, the graves burst open, the dead arise and stream on in endless procession, the great and the little ones of the earth—kings and beggars. Forgiveness strikes fearfully on our ears. The wailing rises higher—our senses desert us. . . . The last Trump is heard. In the silence a nightingale sings, the last echo of the earthly life. The trumpets of the Apocalypse ring out, and a chorus of saints intone 'Thou shall arise.' And behold it is no judgement. There are no sinners, no just. None is great, none is small. Overwhelming love shines. We know and are.

Such a programme might well render impotent the combined powers of musical expression of a Palestrina, a Bach, a Beethoven, a Mahler, with half-a-dozen Pfitzners' thrown in. The symphony was finished in June 1894, when Mahler was within a few weeks of his thirty-fourth birthday; but it had been germinating in his mind for some years. He played the first movement to Hans von Bülow in 1891; and could not find the idea to shape the Finale until, while attending the funeral service in Hamburg for von Bülow, he heard the Klopstock hymn *Aufersteh'n* ('Resurrection'). 'I had searched in all world literature,' he said, 'and the Bible, for the delivering word'; then at the sound of the Klopstock chorale inspiration showed the way.

The 'programme' served for Mahler as the scaffolding of 'extra' musical ideas around which he erected a symphonic edifice. We should endeavour to attend to the work, and aurally 'view' it, more or less as though the scaffolding had not only been taken away but, indeed, has never been there at all. We have seen the ground-plan, the imaginative blue-print, literally with our rational eye. Mahler expects us now to listen to him with the ear of music. He sought to express his nature and being in and through music, not because he was as literary, poetical or philosophical as he was musical; but, on the contrary, because his was a wholly musical consciousness, nerves, mind and emotions. Most of us are able to clarify our questioning about life and death and the meaning of the world—such as they are—in other than musical ways. Mahler, as we must perpetually remind ourselves, especially when listening to the Second, Third, Eighth and *Das Lied von der Erde*, needed to seek through music for the answers constantly prompted by his searching brain and austere culture. He was born in the upsurge of romanticism, and yet he was classically-bred as a musician. Another necessary repetition.

The Second Symphony, for all its appeals to our senses of drama, with its evocations of apocalyptic scenes and sounds, is pretty firmly grounded; the first movement is a bold, quite consequential expansion of first movement sonata-allegro form. The second movement is related to the Minuet, the third a fantasy on the *moto perpetuo:* a Scherzo. And it really merges into the Beethovenish Finale (in form) through an interlude. The third and fourth movements incorporate two *Wunderhorn* songs. Maybe, they disturb symphonic curve or progression; but no more, as far as form considered *a priori* goes, than the preludial storm and subsequent solo recitative disturb in effect the opening-out of the Finale of Beethoven's Ninth. By the rare stroke of apt genius Mahler used, in the third movement, without the words, his *Wunderhorn* song about St Anthony preaching to the fishes after finding his church empty. But when his sermon has been dutifully heard, the fish proceed on their own selfish wicked way: the pike remains a thief, the crab walks backward, the preacher is forgotten. In the Scherzo this ironical allusion points to the sinfulness of man.

The way is perfectly prepared for the contralto song 'Urlicht', of the light which will shine showing the 'eternal life'.

When I first heard the Second Symphony I had no close knowledge of its 'programme'. Yet at the end I needed few important clues: the music told me enough. If there are certain short-circuitings, where the music seems to fall far below the composer's lofty reach, the fault is not a consequence of the effort to describe a 'programme' in a symphony, but because, as I have said, Mahler was not consistently equal to truly lofty musical themes. Yet another point starkly marking him off from Bruckner was this inability to compose a great, 'pure' and sustained tune. By 'pure', I mean a tune not dubiously associated with the familiar, the orchestral, the self-consciously vocal. His genius is most overpowering in his organisation, in his imaginative characters, whether satisfactory or not of pedigree.

The Second Symphony is, for Mahler, objective in conception. There is less of the egocentric man here than in any other of his symphonies, excepting perhaps the Eighth. The reason for so much self-denial was, of course, that in these two works he is possessed by ideas and visions of God, nature, and man's place and destiny in the universe. Apart from a touch of *Schmalz* in the second subject of the first movement, the Second Symphony is almost austerely dramatic or pictorial. The Minuet-*Ländler* movement which follows is gracious and entirely musical. In the Second Symphony Mahler is evolving his art of thematic cross-reference; he takes a phrase out of its first grouping and gives it a particular significance, using it in a different melodic or contrapuntal context. It might not appear in the first place as an obviously definable motif. In the Second Symphony he is also moving towards his device of changing keys progressively from movement to movement. In the First Symphony he has already modulated from a preliminary F minor to a final D major. (The *Lieder eines fahrenden Gesellen* begin in D minor and end in F minor.)

One of Mahler's most enlightened critics, Dr Dika Newlin, has used the phrase 'progressive tonality' to describe Mahler's differentiation of keys from movement to movement ('*Bruckner, Mahler, Schönberg*'; New York, 1947); and Mr Hans Keller, with characteristic nicety of language, prefers the qualification 'progressive' and 'regressive', according to whether the tone sequence moves up or down the circle of fifths. The scholiasts, no doubt, have discovered that Mahler was a systematic tonalist: Mahler, who swore that if he had to set himself deliberately to 'compose', he could never have written a note.

The Second Symphony evolves from C minor to E-flat major; the Fourth from G major to E major; the Fifth from C-sharp minor to D major; the Seventh from B minor to C major; the Ninth from D major to D-flat major; *Das Lied von der Erde* from A minor to C major. Miss Newlin remarks on the half-step accent of the movement sequence of the Fifth and Seventh Symphonies, and suggests that the transitions produce a 'forward impulsion which is synonymous with an optimistic approach to life'. The D to D flat modulation in the Ninth Symphony 'seems to strengthen the feeling of resignation which imbues the work.' Just so; Mahler, we can be sure, hit upon his tone mutations much as a painter goes to work—not looking first at his palette for the colours he needs, but being intuitively led to the right colour or mixture of them. The process is two-way, a reaction constantly going on between conception and material, each inspiring the other by turn; and most times the artist surprises himself into discoveries beyond the powers of reason or theory to anticipate.

First Movement

As usual Mahler opens his Second Symphony with a preludial passage, not a theme for independent use later on, but germinal; parts of it are subsidiary to the main action, accessories after the first movement's dramatic and psychological action, with only two figures destined for consummation in the symphony's development as a whole. This opening section, mainly atmospheric and approximating to a fate-signal or series of signals runs as follows, played by the basses to a sustained string tremolo:

It is a sort of power-house, with these motifs the most combustible as the movement goes on:

1A

1B

These sixteen bars are one of my favourite tests of a listener's understanding of a composer's tone of voice, his identity. I give up anybody as musically uneducated who imagines that this passage has an essential resemblance to the beginning of the prelude to the first act of *Die Walküre* especially during the *crescendo* and *decrescendo* of bars ten to fourteen. Mahler is here using in his own way a device of his period more or less guaranteed, by association, to evoke tension, a hint of wrath to come. A drop of the fifth is the cue for the entrance of the first theme, which we may fairly (and as musicians) call the movement's hero:

2

The melody quickly absorbs the figure from the prelude:

2A

It marches with some decision until a sudden descent:

3

Then a full orchestral cadence, leads to a very *Mahlerisch*, nostalgic melody:

This is followed by the first hints of the 'Resurrection' motif:

5

It is accompanied by the threatening motion in the bass and is attempting a swelling cadence when the dream is broken by a peremptory E-flat minor chord, with a sustained trombone held as threat; and we are at the movement's commanding convulsive beginning again. But now the heroic theme cheers up:

6

followed by a transition momentarily aspiring:

7

We are in the first development (there are two in the movement). I am surprised that neither Bekker nor Specht in their comprehensive examinations of the Mahler symphonies have drawn attention to the fact that the first two bars in the above quotation, Ex. 5, are a harbinger of the 'Resurrection' motif which leads to the apotheosis of the Finale.

The heroic theme vainly resists:

8

A tussle of E-flat major and G minor dissolves; the tread of the cortège recedes and we hear lamentation:

9

The wood-wind echoes; again there is a transition to the nostalgia of Ex. 4, this time in C major. And Mahler does not merely and formally recall it; he makes a fantasy of it, almost a 'Siegfried Idyll', in itself—a musical interlude which does not interrupt the symphonic sequence. He muses ingenuously on these new figures and derivations:

10

11

12

This section alone is ample evidence of the way Mahler improvises without losing grip on his main context as symphonist. To a shadowy march the Idyll fades in the orchestral twilight. And out of it the basses move again, as at the symphony's beginning, but this time they are hesitant, sinister.

13

In a toneless voice a strange visitant announces itself: a sort of *Dies Irae*, disguised, hooded.

14

Mahler, as I insist, does not readily submit to academic X-ray examination. If I am going rather microscopically into the Mahler rationale as I review the symphonies, the intent is not that of the familiar analysis. My purpose is first, to satisfy my own curiosity in Mahler's entirely personal and original way of making a symphony. Second, I hope to lighten the way for those of my readers who are finding Mahler's music for the first time. Also I hope to explode once and for all the notion that Mahler was prolix in a confused, muddled-minded fashion. He was, as a fact, very prolix, leaving little to our imagination. But never was he a loose thinker; on the contrary his processes of musical creation have seldom been surpassed for power of concentrated and allusive thematic synthesis. Analyse, say, a Brahms symphony after you have analysed

Mahler—it is child's play. And, in saying this, I do not belittle Brahms, whose methods were entirely different from Mahler's. There is no obviously Jewish music in Mahler—we have agreed, or haven't we?—none of the familiar Jewish accents. But his race comes out in his many gestures, his quick pin-pointed intelligence—and in his inability to restrain himself. While still in the first development, Mahler works up another climax from the concealed *Dies Irae* motif, and brings it to a head by devices of contrasted accents, rising and descending sequences, all of them tricks of the trade today in any movie-show factory of background music, but not generally worn out in Mahler's superbly expert and vehement control.

The heroic figure tries to get a foothold:

15A

A challenge comes from

15B

The basses press on; and the anapaest motif derived from the symphony's introduction enters with militant stride:

16

This theme takes a turn upward, and now is heard, in D major, the embryo of the 'Resurrection' song of the symphony's Finale:

17

It cannot yet prevail. The rising heroic theme persists, again labouring against the descending forces:

18

At the break of the tonal wave there is a heaving motion recalling the pendulum of the First Symphony; then with a drop of a heart-beat, and a cymbal crash, there is a stampede downwards to a wavelike sequence. A change in the basses from C sharp to C clears the storm, and a pathetic echo of the Ex. 4 'nostalgic' melody dwindles to a rather feminine metamorphosis of the 'Resurrection' cadences:

19

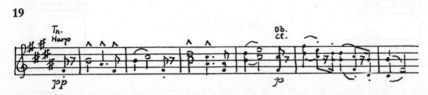

Yet again the drum-crack, and a variation on the symphony's beginning in the basses

20

and the unmistakable *Dies Irae* is heard ironically accompanied by its simulacrum—one of Mahler's finest sardonic strokes. The heroic theme is lured into the procession, and with a sudden aspiration gets a real glimpse of the salvation to come.

21

E

The *Dies Irae* overwhelms this theme at its submissive cadence, and there is another crisis, with a chromatic figure, own brother to the one in the First Symphony, persisting in the storm and stress, which is, for all the melodrama, masterfully steered through the fanfare of

At the last desperate thrust of the heroic theme the orchestra is shattered by yet another chromatic landslide, culminating in *fortissimo* brass and timpani hammering, the most alarming dissonance (up-to-date) in young Mahler's output:

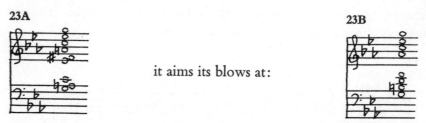

it aims its blows at:

The second development is at an end. The recapitulation is concentrated; C minor again leads to E major for the familiar 'nostalgic' theme, but Mahler's recapitulations are never merely 'recaps'. The lyrical theme is characteristically wheedled into phrases dripping with *Zärtlichkeit*

The coda goes to the grave-side to the tread of

and

25B

The chief mourners are:

26A

and

26B

The gloom and funerary air are intensified by tonic-dominant drum-triplets, and Mahler's major-minor shadings; the coffin is lowered on a C-major triad, which is transformed into a wraith-like C minor. Then the orchestra and all the movement collapses. 'Alles endet, was entstehet'[1] —or as the learned Bekker pithily puts it, 'Das verklärende Bild ist verschwunden.'[2]

The symphony emulates the Beethoven heroic-apotheosis manner of the Ninth Symphony; without an Adagio, maybe, but the spirit and reach are kin.

The Second Symphony is not as closely integrated thematically and rhythmically as the First, where a single interval goes through the whole work, shaping or prompting. The first movement of the Second Symphony certainly refers to the finale by means of the embryonic 'Resurrection' motif and the *Dies Irae*, and a theme subtly extracted from the bass introduction. But these thematic references do not govern the texture essentially; they enter only as potents or heralds. The second movement is an Andante moderato, a charming blend of minuet of eighteenth-century lineage, spiced with the *Mahlerisch* 'nature tone'. So little is it related to the symphony as a whole, either in its atmosphere or in its

[1] All perishes
That exists

[2] The transfigured picture vanishes.

thoroughly composed style, that Mahler himself felt some difficulty in making a convincing transition to it from the mood and method of the first movement. He suggested a pause of at least five minutes—'Eine Pause von mindestens fünf Minuten'. Then he instructed that the next three movements should be played without a break. As a consequence of a want of definitive thematic connection between these three movements, there is a possibility that the casual listener might get the sense of disconnection, or that he has suddenly, after hearing a first movement of portentously symphonic dimensions, been taken momentarily into the more comfortable habitat of a suite. A disconnection of this kind will be avoided if the listener keeps in mind the main psychological (ethical if you like) argument. The Adante should be regarded as 'a blissful moment' of escape, a recollection of distant happiness and innocence.

To return to a summing-up of the rationale of the first movement. The great virtue of it is Mahler's plasticity, especially in his variations of small figures swiftly detached; as an example, his use of the two short and one longer note motif, and the triplet first heard in the bass introduction to the first movement:

27

At the last climax of the movement we hear a brilliantly apt metamorphosis, in a pace and turmoil in which good ideas can easily count for nothing in less than informed ears:

28

and

29

I often wonder why composers take so much trouble. Only a few people in the crowd ever become aware of the many fine touches of art they lend to a tonal momentum, which no doubt would achieve without them a generally exacting and satisfying effect on average audiences. The artist, of course, has his own delight when these subsidiary ideas come surprisingly to him, like—in Goethe's phrase—'children from God'. Nowadays a composer may hear, on a gramophone record, as many performances of his work in a day as Mahler heard of one of his works in a lifetime. He never heard, except in his imagination's ear, the sound of a single note of *Das Lied von der Erde* or his Ninth.

Of all nineteenth-century composers, I repeat (aber, 'nur mit ein bisschen anderen Worten') our *Schmalz* Mahler, long-winded, theatrical, romantic, for ever seeing himself in fatalistic and dæmonic apotheosis, was the most close and allusive musical thinker of them all.

I will anticipate arguments of critics by admitting here and now that it is not difficult to ring changes on the everyday coin of any musical idiom or basic material. Mahler's triplets and military anapaests were the heritage in his memory of youth spent near barracks, where in the distance he heard the bugles. Maybe. He had the genius to translate them into language as subtle, sometimes, as it is personal.

SECOND MOVEMENT

The movement begins with a strain which the uninitiated at first imagines he has heard before, associating it with Haydn, Dittersdorf, or music of their period:

30

Rich and ingenious scoring signs the music 'Mahler' in every ornamented bar, self-consciously gracious. The hard, bony, linear Mahler is forgotten for the time being. This main theme is thrice re-garnished, with diverting short interludes, such as:

31

The Austrian *Lokalton* is heard from the clarinet, followed by the flute and oboe:

32

A gorgeous stretch of string writing occurs when the 'cellos sing with the main theme:

33

Few conductors see to it that these flowing 'cello phrases, in which the instrument wallows, do not over-sound the accompanying minuet motif. The trill and grace-note in the eighth bar of the above example is as lovable as anything in Mahler. There is a *pizzicato* variant of the minuet as entrancing as the most piquant of Tchaikovsky. The movement also captivatingly exploits the device of the repeated short note indicating suspense: 'Wait for it'. Only in the Fourth Symphony does Mahler compose with this geniality and ease. He is actually heard smiling and, though he had a lancing wit, he didn't often smile. No portrait of him that I know shows him smiling. The second movement of the Third Symphony, once so much in favour that it was often played at concerts in Austria and Germany, as a detached piece, is rather contrived in its melody and texture. The minuet of the Second Symphony is on the whole spontaneous, winning, and, to my mind, irresistible in its refined touches of musical art. I admit a certain deliberate ingenuity in the contrasting sections; but, as we have agreed, Mahler could not for long be simple or single-minded. He was always displaying his rich technical assets without reserve. But we can overlook conscious cleverness if now and again, indeed many times, we are given invention, rendered felicitous with genius, such as:

34

THIRD MOVEMENT

Back to the world of the present, fateful and ironic, a scherzo in the manner of a *perpetuo mobile*, with rondo form as basic pattern. The first and third sections absorb the melody and rhythm of the *Wunderhorn* song telling of St Anthony preaching to the fishes. Mahler here does without words but Mahlerians know the text:

> Die Hechte blieben Diebe,
> Die Aale viel lieben,
> Die Krebs geh'n zurück,
> Die Stockfisch' bleib'n dicke,
> Die Karpfen viel fressen,
> Die Predigt vergessen,
> Die Predigt hat g'fallen,
> Sie bleiben wie Allen.[1]

A masterstroke of irony indeed, to use and transform in a symphony dealing with mortal aspiration and mortal proneness to error and temptation the song-fable of St Anthony's vain effort to convert the fishes!

[1] The pike remains thief,
The eel indulges itself,
The crab walks backward,
The stockfish remains stupid,
The carp goes on gorging,
The sermon forgotten,
The sermon's a flop,
Nobody converted.

Only Berlioz has equalled Mahler's sure understanding in this movement of the power of wind-instruments to suggest mockery of simple idealism. To realise fully Mahler's genius for thematic self-quotation and transformation I recommend that this movement is compared with the song, the 'Fischpredigt des Antonius'. Quotation of theme in black and white tells only half of Mahler's sarcastic fantasy, the gusto of it, displayed in this wonderful scherzo-music, entirely original when it was composed some seventy years ago and still sounding original to present-day ears.

Two drums send the movement on its irreverent way with mischievous gurgles from the bassoon and clarinet:

1

The well-known song-themes follow on the heels of each other:

2

Whole tones in the bass! Then we hear what I shall here call the principle *Predigt* (sermon) theme. It is summarily scoffed at later on:

3

A whiff of homeliness temporarily sweetens the air:

The first section of the Scherzo is grotesque with minor tone. Now occurs an F-major episode, but the hurrying rather spectral motion is maintained:

Running on to:

A variant of the opening dance figure, and snatches of the *Predigt*, has a ghostly sustained note by the flute overhead, leading to a sudden fanfare in D major for horns and trumpets:

The gnomic atmosphere comes again in a quasi-fugal variant ending in another assertion of the fanfare which melts into a truly *Mahlerisch* strain of nostalgia from the trumpet—'sehr ausdrucksvoll gesungen'—(from the trumpet, mark you!)

Mahler dwells on this theme, in a sort of trio division, weaving arabesques round it, sharing it amongst harp, trumpet, oboe and clarinet. Now, by another unexpected yet quite logical change, the landscape darkens and out of the twilight we hear the germ of the *Glaube* (faith) motif, which is important in the Finale, a *Deus ex machina*, in fact. A reprise is, as in nearly all Mahler's 'repeats', subtly varied. He told Natalie Bauer-Lechner that according to his principle as a composer development should be continuous, with no more repetition. ('Bei meinem Prinzip, dass sich nichts einmal etwas wiederholen darf, sondern alles aus sich heraus weiter entwickeln muss'.)[1] Yet, as we shall soon see, he understood well enough a classical form's insistence on disciplined recurrence to keep a shapely balance.

The fanfare becomes desperate and the double-basses cannot find a tonic footing in the storm that breaks out. From the sulphurous texture descends:

9

This is a visitant of important and cathartic consequence, which is active again at the beginning of the symphony's Finale. There are spasmodic cuttings-off or suppressions of the *Predigt* theme (another stroke of irony). The *Glaube* harbinger is heard imploring once more. And the movement runs down, note by note as in the beginning, leaving St Anthony deserted, his *Predigt* forgotten. So at one and the same time, Mahler observes classical formal procedure and pungently comments on what the movement has told us as fable. It cannot be stressed too frequently that for all Mahler's extra-musical intentions or implications, his symphonies render unto coded law and order what is their due.

FOURTH AND FIFTH MOVEMENTS

So far, Mahler is leaving us rather much in the air, symphonically and psychologically. After a first movement of large size and gesture, a

---

[1] 'According to my principle, whereby there should be no plain repetition, but all should go forward constantly developing.'

digression has been made to an interlude which in style and content apparently has little to do with its contiguous movements. Also the ironic *Predigt* has obviously landed us with matters needing resolution or consummation. It was permissible, once upon a time, for composers to slip into a symphony a movement—Minuet or Scherzo—delightful in itself as contrast, but of no thematic, let alone psychological, bearing on the work as a whole. With Mahler, each movement is as an act in a play, each carrying the action—symphonic essentially, as well as in its expressive content—a stage further. It was the theory of Paul Bekker that all the symphonies of Mahler press as inevitably from the beginning to the Finale as any drama to its crisis and fate, happy ending or other. It is certain enough that if the Second Symphony had come down to us with only the first three movements composed, we should have been rather at a loss to explain the significance and place in the scheme of these second and third movements.

Mahler goes unerringly to his apotheosis. Maybe—and this is a point we shall find ourselves insisting on again in our studies—he marshals forces not always of the highest thematic calibre. But his shaping, timing; his order of progression and contrasts; his use of vocal and instrumental forces, his power to mount to his height and crown his edifice—here is a dramatic and symphonic synthesis made hypnotic by power of an artist sincere to the point of being obsessed, if not 'possessed', to use the old language, only briefly if suggestively shown to us. He recalls themes with as much symphonic as expressive relevance, the *Dies Irae*, the descending scale of the third movement and figures derived from the symphony's bass-string introduction—these themes are the decisive protagonists of a denouement that evokes a vision of the Last Day, a summons in the world's waste, an emptiness in which we hear only a bird singing. The earth's rabble, beggars and princes go to be judged. Mahler assembles two solo singers, a choir, and enlarges his orchestral forces. Clarinets are made fivefold by addition of two in E flat. To six horns and six trumpets are added four horns and four trumpets, triangle, cymbals, side-drums and kettle-drum (in the distance) and glockenspiel. The orchestra is subdued to a background for the solo contralto, who sings the 'Urlicht' song ('Primordial Light') from the *Wunderhorn* collection, another example of Mahler's genius for natural self-quotation; we feel no hiatus in the general musical texture or diction. Without a break from the third movement, the interlude of the fourth is short and makes not only a transition but a symphonic harbinger of the resolving movement to follow. The soloist, without introduction, intones a poignant quasi-recitative, C minor changing to D flat. A chorale takes up the prayer of the soloist's 'O Röschen rot!' It is played by four horns, three trumpets, bassoon and contra-bassoon. They come to a cadence of an almost parodying piety, for all the world like all the German bands remembered from one's childhood. The hieratic mood is sustained until a Mahler 'hesitant', or 'anticipatory' figure

1

is the cue for the vocal announcement: 'Da kam ich auf einen breiten Weg' ('Now come I upon a broad way'); and a solo violin plays

2

'Da kam ein Engelein und wollt' mich abweisen' ('A little angel came and wanted me to turn back'). There are no fewer than twenty-one changes of the time-signature in thirty-five bars of this highly concentrated movement; yet Mahler creates the proper atmosphere of an eremitic timelessness. The solo voice takes on a human pulsation: 'Ach nein, ich liess mich nicht abweisen' ('No, I did not let myself be turned back').

3

The climax is attained in one of Mahler's most heart-ringing changes; from a passage of quite piercingly anguished semi-recitative, supplication as much as faith,

and from these phrases the closing climax of the movement is built
sequentially.

The crescendo of this 'Urlicht' episode (which somehow and fittingly
is less than a *crescendo*; the tonal pressure is kept beautifully anxious) sends
the solo yearning upwards:

'Will light my way to the blessed life eternal.' The archaic vocal diction,
with an orchestra of monastic and cowled motion, has always sounded in
my ears as one of the most spiritually experienced and composed passages
in all music. I am not a conventional believer—certainly not a church-
man—nonetheless this music has stirred in me almost a solvent to atheism
or philosophic doubt. If it is studied on paper, where the key and *tempi*
modifications have a very contrived look, the art by which it is all done
might seem conscious of what it is expressing and how. But in performance the effect is of a catharsis. All the earlier fret and fever, tension
and anxiety, are as though explained and reconciled to a simple if
trembling trustfulness. The way is clear. But not only humanity is now to
be judged; the symphony itself is in the scales. A failure on Mahler's
part now, a short-circuiting of imagination and execution, and all the
labour and idealism, all the expended musical resources, will run to
futility and vanity.

Mahler does not choose the easy way. There is no immediate choral
peroration. Again, without a break, the finale begins in an orchestral
upheaval: scales, and the double-basses convulsive, as in the first movement. Then a fanfare with descending notes of the third movement now
resolving hopefully:

6

From tremolo bass-strings with harps and horns, slowly rises an annunciatory horn in C major:

7

Falling cadences, tonic and dominant, curtain the scene, then from the orchestra's waste-land (really from 'off stage') come the summons of many horns, blown as though on the wind: the call from the wilderness:

8

As the echoes die, another figure fatefully intrudes over the horn, recalling the triplets of the introduction to the first movement. Indeed, there may be a flashback here to the triplets of the second movement (Ex. 31, p. 70):

9

The symphony is in a waiting world. The *Dies Irae* returns, with *pizzicato* counterpoint of quaver undertones modulating to more fanfares; but again faith is tested. The horn summons is turned into a choral of hope,

10

A new motif, soon to be set to the soprano solo: 'O Glaube!' ('Believe, you were not born in vain'). It is a motif which, in its piercing reiterations and orchestral tremolo, is surely an echo of the agony of Amfortas—though needless to say, Mahler is not thinking of Wagner; he is again, in the musical terms of his period, realising his own ideas:

11

It is music wringing its hands.

Again the *Dies Irae*, in D-flat major, *pianissimo*, solemn in the deepest brass with contra-bassoon. Trombone and trumpet re-assert faith in the resurrection of the body. But for all the consolatory strains, such as

12

and bold *fortissimi* in C major, the music fades. Silence—then a *crescendo* for timpani alone; it is terrific and threatens to shake the orchestra to its foundation:

13

Heavens, fears the uninitiated, the symphony and all the toil and trouble are beginning again! As a fact, we are going into the development-section of a movement which cleverer analysts than myself have mapped out and reduced to a sonata design. We are in the section described by Mahler himself: 'Procession of rich and poor, princes and peasants; a march of the dead to the Judgment.' And here we can admire the parody of the *Dies Irae*.

The theme is a typical example of Mahler's irony; his way of associating a common tune with a tragic or serious musical and expressive event or period.

The march contends against the *Dies Irae*, and is reinforced by a popular music-hall rum-ti-tum. After a stretch of music which frankly is kept going only by rather mechanical rhythmic and rum-ti-tum imitations, we arrive at a climax calling back the first prophecy of the 'Resurrection':

Not yet the goal. With a chromatic slither, the march vanishes. The *Glaube* motif is here elaborated with vehement accumulative sequences, with trumpet calls in the background: a rising sequence to a pronounced fanfare. The descending third movement figure is cut short: Day of Wrath. The next episode is Mahler's most daring and original example of fertilisation of symphony by the dramatic and picturesque: the summons to Judgment:

In the silent vacancy of the orchestra—a silence made more tense by the sound we do hear—a nightingale sings. The sky of the orchestra echoes with trumpet calls. And from the silence comes the 'Resurrection' hymn.

The timing of the entrance of the chorus is a masterstroke. The voices are low:

17

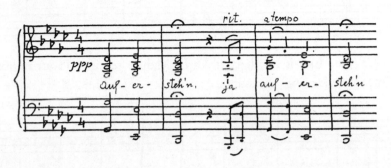

An orchestral interlude divides the hymn, a fantasia on the 'Resurrection' theme. No composer has written out of his heart more devoutly, more trustfully than Mahler here. Yet this movement has been described as 'clap-trap' by eminent critics; and I can see their point. The technique, and our entire view of music and its function, have changed since Mahler's time. And he took risks in the 'Resurrection' apotheosis.

Out of the choral tone rises a soprano, then a contralto; and it is another of Mahler's inspirations so to set them on wing that it is difficult, without eyes on the score, to catch the exact moment of their rising. The 'Glaube' theme is now sung by the contralto solo:

> Glaube, mein Herz, o glaube,
> Es geht dir nichts verloren!
> Hast nicht umsonst gelebt, gelitten
> Dein ist, was Du gesehnt
> Dein, was du geliebt, was du erstritten![1]

These words—and to the hymn's end—are Mahler's own addition to Klopstock's.

[1] Believe, my heart, believe
All is not lost with thee
Hast not lived in vain—
Suffered in vain—!
Thine is what thou hast longed for
What thou hast loved and fought for.

The *pizzicato* bass is another stroke of Mahler tension. From minor to major, the voice sings to assurance:

A violin melody curls round the heart.

The end sets the bells of heaven, and all the Mahler percussion, jubilant, clinching the choir's peroration. The ascent is sturdy.

The end is simple, if not restrained. This is no time for understatement by anybody—let alone Mahler. The organ joins in: tonic and dominant assertions. (Cadence on cadence, winning through to E-flat major.)

As far as conception goes, and as far as execution is concerned, no young man has composed with more than this amount and admixture of original ideas and fresh personal invention. The mingling of a 'programme' with a symphonic form and texture is masterfully if not easefully done. If there is a less convincing integration of theme and rhythmical motives here than we find in the First Symphony, the reason is that Mahler's task in this second symphony was heavier, and in imagination he had grown and developed to a complex of musical, ethical and dramatic impulses and tendencies not to be fused without much hard thinking and intense living day by day—in the spare time, always remember, which he could arrange for himself in the body-and-soul-wearing world of the active, practical and overworked musician.

Symphony No. 3 in D minor

SIX MOVEMENTS

with soprano, contralto and chorus

(1893-96)

IN APRIL 1891 Mahler was appointed first conductor of the Hamburg Opera, and he remained active and masterful in this position for six years. During this period he not only did the work of two men—at one period he was conducting nearly every night—he also worked at the Second Symphony which he had first sketched out in 1887 and, having finished it, composed the Third, one of the longest in existence. At the same time, he wrote several of the *Wunderhorn* songs, and was somehow able to snatch the opportunity to travel to London and conduct *Siegfried* at Covent Garden. His genius did not escape the notice of Bernard Shaw, then music critic of *The World*. 'I have to chronicle several curtain calls for the energetic conductor, Herr Mahler,' he wrote. 'He knows the score thoroughly, and sets the *tempi* with excellent judgment.' (5 June, 1892.) It is an odd thought that Mahler, his brain vibrating with ideas of the Second Symphony, walked about London, perhaps wandering around Southampton Street and Bow Street, at a period of England's musical darkness, when Goring Thomas, Cowan ('The Language of Flowers' orchestral suite), Parry and Stanford, were our most advanced composers. It is conceivable that the musical vision of the Second Symphony's 'Last Trump' overwhelmed Mahler's imagination near Charing Cross.

The Third Symphony is a test of the perfect Mahlerian's devotion. The first movement alone plays for nearly three-quarters of an hour. There are six movements. Originally Mahler planned for the work a seventh, but used it as the Finale and symphonic germ-cell for his Fourth. Once again, he published a programme and withdrew it, still anxious not to be mixed with the 'descriptive' composers. The first programme, necessary for the guidance of his music while creative energy was in full voltage, read as follows:

Symphony III

The Gay Science

A Summer morning Dream

1. Summer marches in
2. What the Flowers on the Meadows tell me
3. What the Animals of the Forest tell me
4. What the Midnight tells me
5. What the Morning Bells tell me
6. What Childhood tells me
7. The Celestial Life

The sixth and final movement is an Adagio, foretelling the Adagio of the Ninth, less subtle in its melodic shaping, though deeply felt and beautifully phrased, with an occasional fullness of harmony that seldom, until the end, visited Mahler. Perhaps, as I have already suggested, he had had no use for it.

In each of his symphonies Mahler explores another realm of imagination, sheds a skin and, as a consequence, evolves, or is on the way to evolving, another technical method, while all the time the Mahler style and progeny remain. Often he leaves the impression that he is making music in sudden upheavals of improvisation, as though, in the middle of a movement, even in the middle of a period, another eruptive idea or emotion has seized him. Here is a reason why this long first movement is usually confusing to the uninitiated; to those listeners who are not experienced in the Mahler way of musical thinking and shaping. Though he most times built his symphonies on a classic ground-plan of sonata form, really his logic and procedure were progressive. His mind did not naturally arrange ideas in A-B-A divisions, clearly defined. A Mahler exposition, development and recapitulation are, as we have seen, subdivided, with many digressions by the way. In the end the various parts or episodes are summed up and made relevant to the whole. The first movement of the Third Symphony is his boldest, most daring— I might as well say reckless—adaptation of sonata form to his perpetually germinating creative impulses. The movement is the symphony's first part; the other five are strongly marked off from it. It contains perhaps the most stupendous and comprehensive expression in all music of the emergence of mysterious natural forces into the abounding, even commonplace, activity of life, unselective but vitally ranging. It is prophetic of *Le Sacre* and Stravinsky. The second and third movements are merely so much 'pretty' and consciously naïve tonal watercolourings.

As well as a soloist for the fourth and fifth movements, with a choir in the fifth, Mahler's orchestra calls for four flutes, four oboes, cor anglais, three clarinets, two E-flat clarinets, bass clarinet, four bassoons, contra-bassoon, eight horns, four trumpets, four trombones, tuba, a battery of timpani (six kettle-drums attended to by two players, or strikers), a Glockenspiel, tam-tam, side-drum, bass-drum, cymbals, triangle, two harps and strings. It is not claiming too much to say that not a semi-quaver runs to waste, as Mahler deploys his orchestral forces.

FIRST MOVEMENT

The first movement is so spacious, so diverse, so proliferating in its energy, as the music awakens from the earth-tone, with horn and trombones sounding through the mountains, shaking the imagination by their associative cadences, that no two analysts have agreed where one 'subject' begins and another ends, no easy task for the anatomist of any Mahler symphony. One learned German authority has stated that the main theme of this first movement extends to three bars only; but another argues that it consists of no fewer than one-hundred-and-three. In his vision of nature, with the 'summer marching in' after the winter's dark caverns of imprisoned life, Mahler conceived his music as undifferentiated at first, the tone emergent, the rhythmic and harmonic motion growing, but in the beginning only plastic and potential. The forgotten Herbert Spencer described biological creation as a development from the homogeneous and simple to the heterogeneous and complex. It is a description which fits this first movement to a semi-quaver.

The movement begins with an introduction nearly two hundred bars long. To the casual ear, the first theme might well sound sufficiently formal and defined, even to the extent of a resemblance to the great tune of the Finale of the First Symphony of Brahms. ('Das sieht jeder Narr', said Brahms when somebody pointed out the resemblance of *his* theme to the one in the finale of Beethoven's Ninth.) Mahler's theme, for all its annunciatory tone declaimed by eight unison horns, cannot quite make up its mind whether it is in D minor or F major:

A

This theme doesn't return in this shape except once, at the beginning of formal recapitulation—there are several quasi-recapitulations on, or by the way. But Mahler gives to it more than one indecorous twist, which should certainly move the Brahmsians to disown it completely. It begets the following vulgar refrain, for instance; no fit company, surely, in a symphony of respectable, not to say, ethical and didactic aspirations:

B

The 'Brahms' theme sinks in a void of changing harmonies

1

The indecisive swaying motion of this figure is a glance forward to the symphony's fourth movement, where the voice sings Nietzsche's words, taken from *Also sprach Zarathustra*: 'O Mensch gib acht, was spricht die tiefe Mitternacht.'[1]

The symphony, after the *Fiat Lux!* of the opening theme, calls up, with solemnly intoned horn invocations, as vivid an impression of a creative if slowly emergent world as any in music. Compared with these calls and cadences, Siegfried's horn is an invocation to Suburbia. Mahler's awakening earth stretches upward thus:

[1] Take heed, O Man, of what the midnight tells!

from the dark backward abysm of

The oboe and clarinet and muted trumpet's leap is one of Mahler's finest strokes of the *Naturlaut*. Echoing in the darkness we hear the horns:

The call is derived from the seventh and eighth bars of the 'Brahms' theme.

A strangely mournful response now resounds out of more subterranean agitation:

These themes, very faintly indicated here in bare quotation, sound like primordial orchestral amoeba; they are not so much developed during the movement as transformed in themselves, without a thematic cross-reference to others. They are as though part of the orchestral womb; I can describe this introduction to the movement only by coining a German word: *Urmusik.*

For some hundred bars horns and trumpets continue their annunciations; Mahler gives them subtle and curiously prophetic intonations, such as:

5

The brass instruments go on perhaps too long with their lonely colloquy. And all the time the orchestra is a cavern of combustible thunder, upheavals and subsidences, spitting and gurglings of lava, always calculated with a superbly acoustical ear. In all Mahler—and if it comes to that, in all symphonic music of the nineteenth century—there is nothing like this introduction for imaginatively calculated tone and dynamics, for suggestions or evocation of primeval parturition, all done with masterfully purposeful orchestral art.

After a chromatic descent the air clears:

6

Wood-wind come in with a flutter of perceptible life; and an oboe sings a plaintive pastoral melody,

7

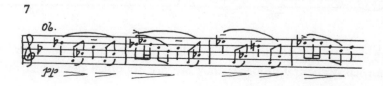

with a solo violin response:

and the basses rumble as though the day—if not the summer—were really beginning at last to march in. There is a flick of quite coy sprightliness in the clarinets:

Now a brisk tread of drums and timpani—but not yet. The funerary rhythm heard at the outset of the introduction is repeated (Ex. 2). The trombones make a fantasia on the calls of Ex. 3, 4 and 5. We are threatened with a recapitulation even before the first movement proper has been reached. Then the fanfares happily modulate to a cadence of hopefulness.

The two main groups do not come together as themes that have been brought up strictly in the old school of sonata development should: each group breeds its own necessary musical or tonal sustenance. On the one hand, the heaving turbulence of double-basses and the stentorian diction of horn and trombone; on the other, the stuff of common day, rhythms and tunes that are all too human. After another chromatic descent, following the cheering-up of the trombones, we hear this common stuff let loose with an unashamed gusto and disregard of all symphonic canon and etiquette. Mahler himself probably drew back in some fear of what he was doing with the art of music, as he composed this movement—'Es ist furchtbar,' he said ('It is frightful'), 'Es sind furchtbare Geburtwehen, die der Schöpfer eines solchen Werkes erleidet, und bevor sich das alles in seinem Kopfe ordnet, aufbaut und aufbraust, muss viel Zerstreutheit, Insichversunkensein für die Aussenwelt, Abgestorbensein vorhergehen. . . .'[1]

[1] 'There are terrible birthpains which the creator of such a work must suffer before his conception is thought out and put into order. He must go through distraction and also become lost to the outside world.'

A symphonic paean to nature's abundancy could scarcely be class-conscious, relegating some themes to the regions of the untouchable. Besides, the ethic and aesthetic aim of the symphony as a whole is to express evolution from inert though fruitful crude material to purification and the shedding of dross. The vulgar tunes of the first movement have their *raison d'être*, symphonically and poetically. Catharsis comes in the last movement.

'Summer marches in.' The lightening of the earth tone; the flutter of Exs. 6 and 9; the pastoral song of Ex. 7, and the basses rumble again, with impertinent trills. It is an accumulation of energy of the over-world, the sane unmetaphysical everyday world. The metre becomes as familiar; it is symphonically 'beyond the pale':

10

With this tune from the clarinets the movement at last definitely gets under way, prancing along to the accompaniment of military fanfares and student choruses.

Now the plebeian course of the music leaves us with little breath left to express our surprise, or horror, that a symphonic movement beginning with so portentous a preludial gesture should gallivant this way:

10A

continuing,

11

the last quotation being a reduction of the pastoral Ex. 8 to the lower orders of Floridsdorf.[1]

'The summer marches in singing and resonant in a way you cannot imagine.' ('Der Sommer marschiert ein, da klingt es und singt es wie Du Dir es nicht vorstellen kannst!') So Mahler wrote to Anna Mildenburg. We can only gasp and wonder at the complex of mind and imagination which, in a symphony setting out to invoke Pan and mysterious dormant creation, should modulate to an embracing human familiarity, after an introduction summoning up seed and protoplasm from a vast, inimical deep. In his subconscious being, as artist, Mahler conceivably might have been influenced in this movement by the first movement of Schubert's C major. There is the preliminary summoning horn call, the adapted *Marche Militaire*, then the solemn invocation of trombones.

Richard Strauss said that this part of the movement reminded him of nothing so much as a procession of the proletariat down the Prater on May Day. Hand in hand with Ex. B swaggers this swaggering 'comrade' of a tune:

12

It swings to a unison rolling and genial end, beer-laden by tuba—and not often is Mahler drunkenly genial:

13

At a first hearing of this music any well-born royal academician of the art might well be forgiven for dismissing Mahler once and for all as a composer of no taste whatsoever. (Mahler, by the way, once took part in a May Day Socialist march in Vienna, with, as he explained afterwards, 'meine Brüder'.)

[1] Working-class district of Vienna.

I agree that Sousa is excellent in his place. None the less, after getting
the wave-length of the movement, I have found a truly convincing power
in the striding bluff familiar refrains. For one thing, the instrumentation,
the setting in which 'summer marches in', is completely apt in every note
not a demi-semi-quaver is superfluous. The trills and fanfares stimulate
picturesque as well as musical fancy:

14

Mahler has not done with the movement yet—far from it. He has
development and reprise to cope with. He handles the vast form easily
and grandly; in no other long movement is he as sure of grasp as here, or
as prolific in ideas.

A surge to a climax follows the amiable tread to the close of Ex. 13.
An upward storm of demi-semi-quavers (Ex. 1A); and eight horns are
again strenuous in the old assertion.

15

This is one of the most astonishing and dramatically quick changes in
music—from the rowdy open-air jollification to the underworld regions.
Eternal recurrence. After such a movement of dangerous symphonic
living, it seems to have been an act of natural consequence that Mahler
chose lines of Nietzsche as the 'guiding word' for a later movement.

Variants on Exs. 3 and 4 make a flash-back once more to the movement's
beginning. A trombone intonation is marked by Mahler 'sentimental':

16

From the distance the English horn echoes Ex. 5, and the solo violin, to trills remembering Ex. 9, plays musingly its solo heard long ago (so it is beginning to seem), Ex. 8. A curious development episode occurs here. I define it as the first part of the symphony's two-fold development-section. In a realm of trills the Brahms-begotten theme (Ex. 10A) is played with; the texture is momentarily spun by a composing Ariel; solo violin and horn make an ethereal fantasy of the ending sentences of the jovial Ex. 13, coming to a close of almost *Schmalz* cadence, punctuated by two-note belly-grunts from the trombones. Next is the awakening of Pan—and the second division of the development. The double-basses dance lumberingly

17

Mahler unreins himself and his orchestra as never before or after. Without an inhibition he enjoys himself. There is even a hint of ironic pedantry during one or two obviously 'worked-out' thematic changes. There are 'oompah' trombones in the corybantic pageant, also a battery of solo kettle-drums. Mahler 'on the Bummel'—

18

Following the gunfire of the drums, the main tune in its first Brahmsian guise is given another fair if momentary hearing; for the recapitulation has set in—and yet another return to the solemn tread of the opening Ex. 2, the trombone still in soliloquy, but now solo. The episode is

shortened; we have already thrice heard the labour-pains of cosmic creation. The trombone goes to a dying fall, rounded off in the 'cellos:

19

Rum-ti-tum in the basses; the march is resumed and audacity takes off its coat. Brahms once more tries to assert himself, and once more he is gathered into the rabble:

20

The swing of Exs. 11 and 12 mingles with the prancing rhythm of Ex. 10. The military fanfares flourish and swagger. The Brahms tune is subjected to a more flagrant depravity:

21

degenerating into

22

The horns blare out sequences apparently incapable of a single blush of shame:

Higher climbs the climax

rolling down full accord to the descent of Ex. 13. Then again the upward *glissandi* rush, threatening yet another return to the trombones of the introduction. But the key of F major is attained in a volley of fanfares, with the lower strings going like mad:

and the percussion cracking. Suddenly the movement is decapitated; cut off in full pelt and fury. As, again, the venerable Bekker succinctly observes: *Schluss.*

Clap-trap? Rather, I would say, sublime puerilities. Only genius can do such things. The movement is alternately stupendous eruption and an extravagant carouse. Hard things have been written of it, even by Mahler admirers. Mr Deryck Cooke, in his excellent B.B.C. monograph on Mahler, describes it as a total formal failure. Mr Desmond Shawe-Taylor, in the *Sunday Times* of 31 January 1960, dismissed it as an 'artistic monstrosity'. On a first hearing I myself suffered embarrassments; but, as I came really to know the movment, by sound as well as by score, the music grew on me. Under the deliberate show of common tunes and rhythms there is a remarkable power of imagination, of musical conception, propelling changes and contrasts; and the intense sincerity is finally overwhelming. This is his vision of an awakening world. He tried to symphonise (God forgive the word!) nature in one embrace of mind and heart, an embrace of awe, gusto, living kindness and reverence. 'It begins as lifeless nature,' wrote Mahler to Anna Mildenburg, 'and rises to divine love.' He was referring to a symphony in the whole, from this riot of a first movement to the benedictory closing Adagio.

It is true that an artistic expression of vulgarity should not end in vulgarity. As Doctor Johnson put it, a man driving fat oxen need not himself be fat. The alleged commonness of sections of this first movement are not expressed by a common, but a highly personal, art. We have, I hope, grown out of the nineteenth-century obsession of symphonic pomposity and piety of diction. Mahler could be pious enough at the right moment, for instance, in the Adagio Finale of this same symphony. But he was, as usual, far-seeing in his effort to clear the symphonic mind of cant. He reached forward in this abused movement to the less pretentious temper of today—and, paradoxical as ever, he glorified the unpretentious at times pretentiously. You need to have come to love this movement to listen to it throughout without impatience and, indeed, without embarrassment. The musical resource, the plenitude of orchestral ideas, conquer in the end. At least, this has been my own experience. 'A total formal failure?'—but it is a movement based on a recognisable sonata-form blue-print: Introduction, exposition, development and a telescoped recapitulation. Mahler while building 'his world' out of symphony was always on his guard against the charge that he at bottom was a composer of programme music; he consequently paid more homage to formal procedure than was necessary. Those critics who find in this first movement a sense of obstructive reprise that holds up the march of summer on its way in—no doubt they have an arguable case. Mahler varies his repeated sections, no doubt; the trouble is that a fanfare can sound much the same the more it is changed.

Perhaps the most historic comment ever passed on the work, exceeding in severity even the censure of Mr Shawe-Taylor and Mr Cooke, was long since recorded by Richard Specht. It was uttered after the first performance in Vienna, by the music critic, Felix Salten. 'Für so was verdient der Mann ein paar Jahre Gefängnis.' Translation here would be a spoilsport.

SECOND MOVEMENT

So far Mahler has been coping with inanimate nature in the raw, in seed, rock, soil, also with human nature in the mob. He turns now to the flowers and beasts of the field, to the world animate and vegetable. The second movement is, in Mahler's own words, the least burdened with labour that he ever composed—it is his *Blumenstück*—'Es ist das Unbekümmerteste, was ich je geschrieben habe'. He didn't usually write at his best during periods when his dæmon rested. This movement, a Minuet Rondo and Variations, and the next, the third, are more 'absolute', more continuously patterned as self-subsistent music, than anything else in his *corpus*. The 'flowers' are sometimes artificial; and only a recurrent note of melancholy (E minor and F-sharp minor) saves the music from prettiness. Mahler actually referred to the movement in terms amusingly portentous: 'Freilich bleibt es nicht bei der harmlosen Blumenheiterkeit, sondern plötzlich wird alles furchtbar ernst und schwer; wie ein Sturmwind fährt es über die Wiese und schüttelt Blätter und Blüten, die auf ihren Stengeln ächzen und wimmern, als flehten sie um Erlösung in ein höheres Reich.'[1]—

It is not easy to understand how Mahler, having encompassed the vastness of the first movement (whatever its faults it is naturally elemental in its range) could modulate to the rather mincing self-conscious charm of

It sounds like a contrived echo of the spontaneous beginning of the second movement of the Second Symphony. I admit the graciousness and ingenuity of the orchestration, and the change of *tempi* and phrasing of the *Blumenstück*, as a whole. But in my ears the lilt is mannered; moreover some periods sound a little old-fashionedly reminiscent of the

[1] Of course, the carefree, cheerful world of flowers does not prevail, suddenly the atmosphere changes—it is dark and heavy. A whirlwind sweeps over the meadow shaking the leaves and blossoms so that they groan and whimper as though crying for salvation.

Flowers Suite popular in the eighteen-nineties (and seldom does Mahler anywhere sound old-fashioned). The movement has often been played at concerts as a piece in itself, taken out of context.

The minuet theme comes to a full close, then a nimbler but still rather contrived counter-motif, follows:

2

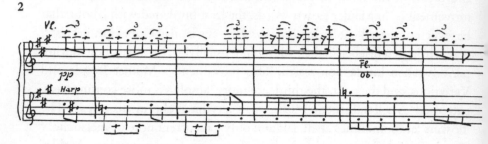

A luscious perfume of summer *Schmalz* comes over the meadows:

3

with harp arpeggios. The minuet is continued, ending coyly thus:

3A

Summer wind ripples the grass:

4

Changing to a dance gently bucolic:

I can only tentatively suggest that the *furchtbar* and *schwer* passages in Mahler's imagination were Ex. 4 and the variation beginning:

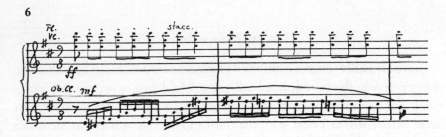

The course of the movement is quite formal. The themes quoted return in the order of their first presentation, in varied dress or decoration.

The suggestions of *Schmalz* of Ex. 3 are mingled with the minuet again. A solo violin joins in the tripping Ex. 5; a languorous horn makes melancholy as the minuet swoons to an end, with solo violin weaving arabesque figures and the expected curtseying cadence. The themes go through no really symphonic changes; as they reappear, Mahler titivates them with all his instrumental wardrobe. In an orchestral suite the music could give pleasure and not leave us feeling a lack somewhere, as in this ambitious earth-to-heaven-ranging symphony it certainly does. It is all too ingenious in its blandishments. I do not feel happy as Mahler combines naïvety and deliberate artifice, putting on all his jewellery at once. The movement's permanent interest is in the texture, finely-spun and prophetic, of enchantments soon unmistakably to come.

The symphony might well seem a strange mixture of styles, unless this movement, and the third, are heard and regarded as an interlude, the context of the whole work never forgotten. Mahler divided the symphony into two parts, intending the first movement (in his long view) to serve as the first part of an entire concert, the second part to be played after the interval, consisting of movements two to six.

In my own shorter view, the second and third are bridge-passages to a resumption, in the fourth movement, of the truly symphonic argument.

Clearly the second and third movements are as a 'point of rest'. Symphonic balance would more satisfactorily have been obtained with a shorter third movement, where the repetitions of the post-horn are academic. Better still might the symphony have gone its course if the flowers and beasts could have made their communications, told their tales, in one movement. Fortunately, each of the inner movements are, for Mahler, very short; and in any case, who am I and who are we, to tell Mahler how to compose a symphony?

THIRD MOVEMENT

I have probably written captiously of the *Blumenstück*. It can be endearing, when one is in the mood; but I am not a Mahlerian who can habitually relish our composer's deliberately evoked naïvety. Possibly I shall now seem harder still as I deal with the third movement, a Scherzo, in which he uses an early *Wunderhorn* song:

> Kuckuck hat sich zu Tode gefallen
> An einer hohlen Weiden.
> Wer soll uns diesen Sommer lang
> Die Zeit und Weil vertreiben?
> Ei, das soll tun Frau Nachtigall,
> Die sitzt auf grünem Zweige,
> Sie singt und springt, ist allzeit froh
> Wenn andere Vögel schweigen.[1]

A foretaste is here of Mahler's liking for minor and major exchanges and combinations. But I find the material much too much of a piece to sustain a symphonic movement. The trio, with its wonderfully intoned post horn, coming from the man-made world and quietening the gambols of the animals, is an inspiration, though Mahler overdoes it, in another academic offering or genuflection to sonata-formal repetition. He was, as we have already seen and noted, constantly eager to prove himself an

---

[1] Cuckoo has died in a hollow willow. Who will pass the time for us during this long summer? Ah, it must be lady nightingale, sitting there on the green bough. She sings and springs, is always gay, when other birds are silent.

'absolute' musician—to use the hallowed term of his period. The main themes are

The flute has a playful tailpiece to the motif:

Three trumpets and 'cellos sustain a minor mode dance fantasy:

The give-and-take of tonality, goes on simply and persistently:

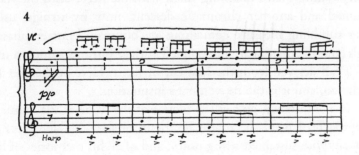

We are beginning to think we are listening to another version of the 'Casse-Noisette' suite. Tediousness sets in:

A change of grouping and phrasing animates the scene:

The stamping dance is here again, with trills in the wood-wind and strings, leading back to the 'cuckoo' song:

Violin figuration runs along to another bout of the stamping dance, this time made ponderous by stomachic trombones. A chromatic descent brings in a sort of fantasia section, in which Mahler plays with the motifs, counterpointing them, tinselling them with the harp, until the stamping is resumed and another chromatic descent, now by strings, ushers in another rumbling measure containing an 'oompah' brass emphasis. The animals (and the theme) are interrupted at their fun and games; a trumpet makes a call derived from the first bar of Ex. 1. Here begins the Trio of the Scherzo, and it is the movement's inspiration.

Out of the distance, and in the silence of the scene as the animals hear the approach of man—he might be friend or foe—Mahler plays on the post-horn, with sustained string notes; and of all his memories of barrack bugle-blowings of his childhood none stirred him to more haunting intonation.

Post-horn in B

The animals listen timidly:

Again the post-horn sounds, coming nearer, the horns now making an old-world and lovely cadence. A final fanfare, then the dancing is revived, after some misgivings. Now we get a succession of figure variations, such as:

The stamping motif fortifies the animal's courage, bass-tuba and trombones grunting:

12

A recapitulation with quite academic changes of rhythm and orchestration and dynamics suddenly ends in the familiar Mahler upward harp *glissando*. An E-flat minor *fortissimo*, then the heavens open—as they open in the Adagio of the symphony to follow, the Fourth—much the same horn call and formula, original and unmistakable. We even hear echoes in the trumpets from the 'Resurrection' episode in the Second Symphony.

After this strangely apocalyptic occurrence in so innocent a movement the animals scamper to the end in a bustling conventional coda.

FOURTH MOVEMENT

'What the midnight tells'. The beasts of field and forest have hinted at knowledge of fear; and even the flowers in the meadow have bent and been broken in the wind. But only man is conscious of the sadness of the world and of his loneliness in it. To tell us of this, Mahler uses the 'Nightsong' from Nietzsche's *Also sprach Zarathustra* as the guiding, liberating word for his musical inspiration:

> O Mensch!
> Gib acht!
> Was spricht die tiefe Mitternacht?
> Ich schlief, ich schlief!
> Aus tiefem Traum bin ich erwacht!
> Die Welt ist tief!
> Und tiefer als der Tag gedacht!
> Tief ist ihr Weh!
> Lust—tiefer noch als Herzeleid!
> Weh spricht: Vergeh!

Doch alle Lust will Ewigkeit!
Will tiefe, tiefe Ewigkeit![1]

Mahler sometimes builded wiser than he knew.[2] This fourth movement
begins with a reference, surely, to the 'inert nature' motif of the symphony's introduction (see Ex. 1, p. 86):

and

and

[1] 'O man, take heed, what saith the midnight, I slept my sleep. From deepest dream
am I awakened. The world is deeper, deeper than the day could tell. Deep is man's woe;
joy—deeper still than grief. Woe speaks: Hence! For joy wants all eternity, wants deep
profound eternity.'

[2] Bekker quotes a conversation in which Mahler said of his Third Symphony:
'Aus den grossen Zusammenhängen zwischen den einzelnen Sätzen, von denen mir
anfangs träumte, ist nichts geworden, jeder steht als ein abgeschlossenes und eigen-
tümliches Ganzes für sich da: Keine Wiederholungen, Reminiszenzen. Nur am
Schluss des "Tierstückes" fällt noch einmal der schwere Schatten, den am Ende der
Einleitung die leblose Natur, die noch unkristallisierte, unorganische Materie lastend
wirft. Doch bedeutet sie mehr einen Rückfall in die tierischen Formen der Wesenheit,
ehe sie den kolossalen Sprung zum Geiste im höchsten Erdenwesen, dem Menschen, tut.'
('The great unity of movements which I dreamed of has come to nothing. Each of them
is sufficient unto itself. No repetitions, no reminiscences. The shadow which nature, form-
less and unresolved, casts at the end of the introduction, recurs just once more at the end
of the Tierstück. The symphony returns to the dark animal forms of existence, before
it takes the immense leap to the spirit of the highest being—mankind.'

Then there is the Mahler *Naturlaut*—the 'nature sound':

and the theme of *Lust die Ewigkeit* which goes as follows:

I cannot think that this theme has nothing in common with the bodeful call in the introduction to the symphony:

No Mahler commentator has drawn attention to this flash-back. It is psychologically as well as symphonically pertinent, entirely in tune with the significance of the 'O Mensch' recitative, as it merges on the violins from the deeps of the orchestra, beginning 'inertly', then rising slowly to some effort of annunciation, sung by the contralto.

The *Lust die Ewigkeit* sung by a voice tells us that from the void mankind has emerged, singing of some hope in the darkness.

A solo violin adds a pathetic note of comfort, recalling the 'Da kam ein Engelein und wollt mich abweisen' episode in the 'Resurrection' Symphony.

Out of these bare themes Mahler makes his movement of transition to the symphony's apotheosis. It is a subtly modulated orchestral and vocal monotone, at a first hearing perhaps repetitive; but on close acquaintance, it is heard as an inevitable way of approach to what is now to come.

'Doch alle Lust will Ewigkeit—will Ewigkeit'

intones the voice, then the orchestra sinks back to the darkness.

FIFTH AND SIXTH MOVEMENTS

With a transformation of surprise and felicity we are conscious of the singing of the boy angels:

There is the tolling of a heart-easing bell. Mahler asks the cherubim to produce from their lips a humming sound, making the most of the consonant *M*. This is no conventional heavenly choir; no echoes here from the earthy pew. To the accompaniment of the 'bim-bam', young women sing a song in the *Wunderhorn* vein:

Es sungen drei Engel einen süssen Gesang;
Mit Freuden es selig in dem Himmel klang,
Sie jauchzten fröhlich auch dabei,
Das Petrus sei von Sünden frei.
Und als der Herr Jesus zu Tische sass,
Mit seinen zwölf Jüngern das Abendmahl ass,

Da sprach der Herr Jesus, was stehst du denn hier?
Wenn ich dich anseh', so weinest du mir!
Und sollt' ich nicht weinen Du gütiger Gott,
Ich hab' übertreten die zehn Gebot'.
Ich gehe und weine ja bitterlich.
Ach komm und erbarme dich über mich.
Hast du denn übertreten die zehn Gebot',
So fall' auf die Knie und bete zu Gott,
Liebe nur Gott in alle Zeit.
So wirst du erlangen die himmlische Freud'.
Die himmlische Freud' ist eine selige Stadt,
Die himmlische Freud', die kein Ende mehr hat!
Die himmlische Freude war Petro bereit't
Durch Jesum und Allen zur Seligkeit.[1]

The boys' 'bim-bam' ceases for only a few of the hundred-and-twenty bars which are (for Mahler) the movement's 'heavenly length'. The contralto solo expresses Peter's remorse:

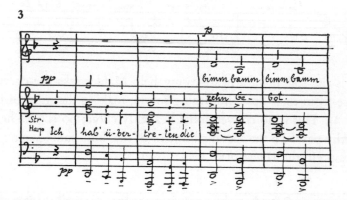

This refrain we shall hear in the closing movement of the Fourth Sym-

[1] Three angels sang a sweet song—the sound to heaven rises. Jubilant they are since St Peter is free of sin. When Jesus with his twelve apostles sat down at the table for his supper, he said: Why are you standing here? I look at you—and you cry! Should I not cry, my benevolent God, I have broken the Commandments. So I must take my leave and cry bitterly. Oh come and take pity on me! If you have broken the Commandments, then fall on your knees, and pray to God. And ever after give God your love, then heavenly joy will be yours. Heavenly joy is a beautiful gift, heavenly joy is never ending. The heavenly joy which St Peter knows he received through Jesus and Grace was everywhere.

phony; and in each place it comes in with a felicitous relevance. No violins are heard in this movement, in which pain and mortal error are sounds coming from a distance left for ever behind. The blending of the boys' and the women's voices, in their different parts, appealing to the picturesque senses and also touching deeper emotions, is effortless. Here Mahler shapes a variation sequence with beautifully shaded textures, and here, if ever, his art is unselfconsciously put to a lovely imaginative purpose. The 'bim-bams' die away; and now we are at the crucial moment and movement. If Mahler should fail now, after all the labour and longitude we have been through! He doesn't fail; or if the height is not scaled, if divine love is not to be told in Mahlerian numbers, the reach is noble and, as I feel it, very moving. If ever a composer sang out of a full heart it is here. Without a break we are listening to the symphony's Finale. The transition is benefactory.

A choir of strings softly begin a prayerful song. It has a good ancestry; the first four bars once on a time reminded me of the beginning of the slow movement of Beethoven's Op. 135 Quartet:

The markings are *Langsam. Ruhevoll. Empfunden. Sehr gebunden, sehr ausdrucksvoll gesungen.* Though the expressive intent is to tell us of heavenly love, the music is not spiritual; it has none of Bruckner's piety. Mahler is on his knees in gratitude for what life has meant for him, reverent for beauty, aching in his heart with the effort of annunciation.

Unmistakably *Mahlerisch* is the next phrase, suddenly touched with his own curve of melody:

He is as much Mahler in his obeisance as in his thankfulness.

A hopeful turn, a Schubert echo maybe, soon takes on a familiar tension

The notes bracketed (A) are prophetic of the Mahler fluid tonality to come, and of the freedom from a central key tyranny; it is also prophetic of the original part-writing of the posthumous Adagio of the Tenth Symphony; nothing like this was to be heard in symphonies circulating at the time of the composition of Mahler's Third. Though this Adagio tells of 'love', no flush of eroticism enters; there is no erotic music in Mahler. Of course, I can't rationalise this opinion or demonstrate its

validity in words; it is a purely personal and sensory reaction. The first
section dies away in cadences which, however, do not come to a full
close but merge into other onward-moving phrases, in the following
manner:

Continuing:

The swaying notes derive from the four bracketed notes in Ex. 2A.
A chromatic change to a development section is heralded by the horns:

Horn
in F

the strings rising in sequences which become strenuous.

5B

A climax brings back disturbances of the first movement:

6

But the storm is calmed after a sustained dissonance.

7

This is the self-pitying chromaticism of Mahler which often caused the lamented Eric Blom to feel queasy in the stomach. It modulates to a return of the main theme (Ex. 1). After four bars it is gently agitated by a Mahler *appoggiatura* which, in the subsequent symphonies, we shall hear time after time:

8

It wrings its heart, not now in any tension, but with a tender sentiment

that should be capable of touching the imagination even of anti-Mahler-
ians, if they could 'see' Mahler at his work, in love with the beauty of the
world:

9

But the musical brain of Mahler is active enough throughout, changing his
themes tonally and contrapuntally. Immediately there is a return to the
swaying Ex. 4, but now a solo violin sweetens it:

10

Continuous variation brings a bridge-passage perhaps tending to get
mechanical in its sequences:

11

A climax of harsh antithetical tone forces is reached, anticipating (years
in advance) the great crisis of the first movement of the Ninth Symphony
('Wie ein schwerer Kondukt') an intensification of Ex. 6. But the Denying
Spirit knocks at the door only to renounce itself. Mahler has now won
through to as much peace of mind as he is ever to know.

H

12

The movement seems to surge to the clinching song of self-mastery at last:

13

But as we anticipate the fulfilment of the main prayer (Ex. 1) there is a chromatic descent of the full orchestra,

14

mounting once more, for the last time, to a great wave mingling echoes of past struggles and present faith and fear:

15

It is a climax as much called for by needs of symphonic as of psychological balance. The trumpets foretell the great apocalypse of the Adagio of the Tenth Symphony. The apotheosis has been attained at last. The main theme strides in confidently on the trumpets, after the last pathetic response in the high wood-wind to the apparently engulfing subsidence of the *Mit höchster Kraft*:

16

The long work is done. All the themes pass by in sequential procession to a full-blown coronation of orchestral sound. The coda, with its persistent drum cracks and D major, goes on too long with elephantine tubas. Mahler, as the reader will have realised by now, had not much reticence. As a whole, the movement is one of the great Adagios in the nineteenth-century manner. The course of the music, self-evolving (save for the one contrived transition passage which I have already noted) was quite original among symphonic composers of Mahler's period. No matter how much difference a listener might find in the material contained in the two works, this Adagio in its thinking and emotional processes is in the lineage of the 'Eroica' of Beethoven. Mahler, of course, could not sustain the heroic gesture; and was none the worse for that. I myself lived the biblical three-score-and-ten before opportunity came my way to know this Third Symphony note by note. Such is the wastefulness of public concerts. For all its short-circuitings, the current of it is genius. And it is the music of a good man. Vain maybe, to dream of making a symphony equal to an encompassing of all nature, with love the universal seed and flowering heaven. 'Ah but a man's reach should exceed his grasp!'—and of no composer more than Mahler can this old-fashioned cry of Robert Browning be echoed.

Symphony No. 4 in G major

FOUR MOVEMENTS

with soprano solo

(1899-1900)

M AHLER COMPOSED THE Fourth Symphony at a time when he was as happy as a man of his physical and psychological make-up well could be. That is to say he had come to some integration and balance as man and artist. In 1897 he was appointed Director of the Wiener Hofoper, and his health was, for him, unusually undisturbed. The world of music lay at his feet. Moreover, his experiences as creative and technical musician had been enriched by the composition of the first three symphonies. He now commanded an orchestral language second to none; he understood as no other composer of his day, and few since, the character, the native speech, of every instrument. He could, in fact, write for orchestra and voice as easefully and as instinctively as a man talks, walks or breathes.

In the Fourth Symphony he found for a while some fulfilment. It is a symphony which contradicts the general view taken of Mahler: in it are no cosmic gestures, no wrestlings with beasts, spiritual or other, no technical miscalculations, or, at any rate, only one; and no tonal excess. No doubt Mahler came to some peace of imagination by what in the latest jargon is called escapism. The Fourth Symphony conjures up a realm of child and youth fantasy, a cloud-cuckoo land. It is a pastoral symphony to begin with, which modulates through a parodying evocation of the grotesque, through the hushed aisles of one of the most beautiful of slow movements, to a simple song-finale in which the birds of the air and a Noah's Ark of animals hurry in expectant chatter to the heavenly feast; where, to words from *Des Knaben Wunderhorn*, the angels bake the bread, and a thousand *Jungfrauen* dance, Saint Ursula herself laughing, while Saint Peter looks on benignly. 'Kein Musik ist ja nicht auf Erden'—no earthly music sounds here. Mahler, in his Fourth Symphony does not strain his expressive scope; his orchestra is reduced considerably in numbers. He claimed that the symphony contains no *fortissimo*, and he added that people who imagined that he could compose only with a tonal battery would be astonished 'In der ganzen Symphonie kommt, entsprechend seinem Gegenstand kein einziges Fortissimo vor— darüber werden sich die Herren, die immer behaupten, ich arbeite nur mit den stärksten Mitteln, wohl verwundern. Ja, in der ganzen Vierten fehlen die Posaunen.'

The basis of the Fourth's orchestral texture is the strings. So far, especially in the Third Symphony, Mahler has concentrated on the wind-instruments, which have conditioned much of the thematic material, with a final peroration of brass climax, fanfares and a large range of dynamic. Here, in the Fourth, the strings weave and shape the main outlines and patterns, revelling in decorations and *portamenti* born of a luscious response to the possibilities of warmth and poise of string melody. The wind are used to tint the texture, or to come singing through it, often with a Schubertian tenderness; or they make the noise of lowing oxen, or the chirping of birds. And the Mahler timpani abstain moment-arily from thunder and titanic fist-blows of percussion; they echo the atmosphere of the 'celestial life', open the doors of the child's paradise, every sound serving strictly musical and symphonic purpose.

This happy and realised Fourth Symphony was not produced, we can be sure, mainly because Mahler was as man and musician enjoying a few years of peaceful integration of his mixed and very human elements. The imagination of an artist essentially 'romantic' (to use the helpful cant-word of the present-day) does not set to work entirely governed by material influences acting upon him either directly or indirectly. He is very much, as an artist, influenced by reactions of the inner man and his imagination. After the Second Symphony, which told of man's brief portion on earth and of the blessed Resurrection; and after the Third's tremendous reach, straining to grasp all nature, all life, animal, mineral, vegetable and spiritual, there was bound to be a subconscious release of tension. Besides, during the composition of his Third, Mahler was, I believe, moved in the direction of the vastly different imaginative and tonal habitat of the Fourth by one of those inexplicable chances which sometimes give a turn or twist leading to an artist's next step or transition.

We have seen that originally the third symphony was planned to have a seventh movement bearing the title 'Was mir das Kind erzählt' ('What Childhood tells me'). Obviously such a movement could not go in a symphony already dealing in its fifth movement with much the same idea; for Mahler's conception of childhood was one bound to involve celestial clouds of glory. Besides, a fanciful not to say whimsical Finale to the Third Symphony would have made for complete anti-climax. Out of the rejected seventh movement of the Third came the conception of the Fourth.

The 'angel' movement of the Third and the Finale of the Fourth, both make elaborate use, as connecting refrains, of a phrase taken from the song, *Wunderhorn* in style and feeling, 'Es sungen drei Engel'. This song is generally supposed to have been written well in advance of the composition of the Fourth Symphony. And the *'Wunderhorn'* song which is the main foundation of the Fourth's Finale, called 'Wir geniessen die himmlischen Freuden', dates from March 1892. According to Bekker, the *Engel* verse used in the fifth movement of the Third Symphony was set to music primarily composed for the symphony, and was not a self-quotation. ('Mahler hat das nächstfolgende Wunderhornlied nicht aus einer früheren Komposition herüber genommen in die Sinfonie, sondern es eigenst hierfür geschrieben.')[1]

Curious, indeed, then that in both the *Himmlische Freuden* and the *Engel* setting, this refrain comes aptly in, first to these words:

A

then to these

B

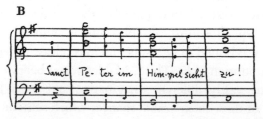

[1] 'The *Wunderhornlied* in this symphony is not taken from an earlier work but was composed specially for it.' Mahler confessed that the appearance of the same theme in the fourth movement of the Fourth Symphony and the fifth of the Third was surprising to himself—'das es ihn selbst befremd'—see *Errinnerungen an Gustav Mahler* by Natalie Bauer-Lechner.

Bakker's theory is that the Finale of the Fourth Symphony thematically, and as far as significant content goes, contains the germ-cells of the entire symphony and that, so to say, we should hear it with the end foreseen at the beginning. I find this a far-fetched notion. Mahler, as I have suggested, possibly had his imagination swayed to his next symphonic course by contemplating the movement rejected from the Third, rejected or held back in the actual writing of it. It is wisest, though, to listen to the Fourth Symphony without any sort of forward and backward glances interchanging mentally. Here, at any rate, is a Mahler symphony which can be appreciated in an exclusively musical way, without programmatic implications distracting our absorption in music abounding in melody, rich and original in its part-writing, fanciful and witty in its transitions of key, and beautifully shaped in its changeful course to the appointed end.

FIRST MOVEMENT

The first movement is an astonishing blend of naïvety and subtlety. Melodies simple and lilting as folksong are played with and shaped into symphonic form and texture with acute musical logic, yet it is all without, or nearly without, the Mahler sophistries. The movement begins by a statement or exposition of no fewer than five melodies, each in itself a musical organism. Here is no easily mapped territory, no A-B-A sonata fingerposts. The movement is really an elaborate Rondo, with not one but at least five themes recurring, never in quite the same notes. I say 'at least' because so cunningly does Mahler transform a melodic shape or rhythmical period that in any text-book thematic analysis of this movement the saving phrase 'E. & O. E.' should be printed. For instance, in the development section we hear the motif of the Child's Paradise.

1

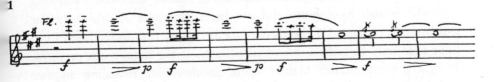

Now, knowing Mahler as I do, I am not prepared to say that this happy young tootling did not come from

2

which is a typical grown-up Mahler 'cello melody marked *espressivo* and *Ton!* The symphony is, in fact, a mingling of Mahler boy and man. The opening song of the symphony, gay and jaunty, for strings only,

3

is agitated in the first movement's development into:

3A

And, in the slow movement, this artful artless phrase is transformed into the Mahler fingerprint of nostalgia, not to say self-pity:

3B

I have known musicians and conductors of Mahler who have lived long with the Fourth Symphony and not been conscious of this particular and protean change. Of the development of this first movement, I can hope here only to print a sort of map showing the main roads or paths. In nearly every period Mahler opens another gate revealing another path leading to a fresh vista. Dr Redlich has described, once and for all, this original and mazeful development: '. . . prodigious wealth of themes and motifs cropping up ceaselessly . . . only to become completely transformed and often to be reshuffled like a pack of cards.' To fall back on my own language, the development of this first movement is as though thematic changes are seen through the Looking-Glass: the melodies and rhythms grow and they diminish; they scuttle underground like rabbits. For instance, this figure:

which falls down all the stairs of the orchestra to the cellar of the contra-basses. Or the themes appear now in extension, now in shorter shapes, Mad Hatters and March hares. But every note, I insist, is governed by strict musical purpose, sure feeling for symphonic procedure.

The movement begins with a jingling figure reminiscent of sleigh-bells or fowl-yard clucking, according to your fancy. This figure is used as a bridge passage several times in the movement, and is the *ritornello* joining together the changes of the Finale; where, of course, it is transformed in scoring and in its shaping.

(The onward motion of the quavers and semi-quavers persists almost throughout the movement; it is obviously going somewhere.) Now the movement's main song comes in, gracefully poised (Ex. 3.) and it is lustily answered, by 'cellos and 'basses over a wind tintinnabulation derived from the first two bars of Ex. 4:

The rising dotted figure at A is a prominent counterpoint throughout the movement. Violins play it downwards—another busy if repetitive factor in the development:

and as the lower strings rise up buoyantly again, the main song sets off once more, beginning with a charming canon for violins and 'cellos:

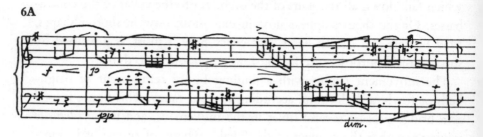

If I write down every note in the chain of the exposition's themes, to avoid a missing link, I shall be bound to write out the score in full.

A transition brings in a more bucolic accent:

It is a dance of child-like expectation, and it runs to the dominant down hill merging into a truly *gemütlich* striding tune marked *breit gesungen* and *Ton!*:

This theme has a warm lovable counterpart—here Mahler composes with an ease and fullness of harmony not surpassed in all his output; no torment or strain in this full-hearted music:

9

It is quite profane to reduce such music to short score. A tail-piece, humorously archaic, half-closes the exposition:

9A

But the sleigh-bells sound again and now the main song with the rhythmic dotted notes of Ex. 5, varied in combination, lead to a coda of *Mahlerisch schwärmerei* definitely ending the exposition in these lovely cadences:

10

and

10A

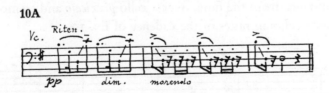

What we have heard so far is a sequence of episodes joined by the introductory jingling motif, a set of quasi-symphonic variations. The development begins with another return of the 'sleigh-bells' (this term I use merely as an identifying phrase, for there is nothing wintry in this symphony). A lower string mounts upward, kin to Ex. 5 (at A). A solo violin spins a high web of gossamer. The landscape grows misty in E minor. Then Mahler takes the major theme, cuts it in two, and makes the seventh bar begin as though a fresh statement, with what has so far been the symphony's first theme.

11

Erwin Stein neatly described this transformation as 'what has been subsidiary becomes the main substance and the first idea becomes an afterthought.'

The main theme tries to get its independence back as it yearns upward:

12

But there is an octave collapse, a scurry to cover, in a descending octave, and tremolo short notes. A bass *pizzicato*, trills in the 'cellos, and we have come to the symphony's Pisgah sight. Out of the distance we hear the call to the Child's Paradise, far away yet but unmistakable. In the Finale we hear it strained of earthiness, changed to the first phrase of the song of heavenly plenty. Here it is an eager boyish call, nothing more, sounding in a high distance from the flute, over a 'cello *pizzicato* and tremolo, with a bass clarinet echoing notes of the cadence of Ex. 10.

13

I first heard this passage at a rehearsal in Manchester—the Hallé Orchestra conducted by Hamilton Harty. I then knew nothing of the symphony's expressive purpose. But at once the high flute over the plucked deep strings brought to my imagination a picture of some piping from a far horizon, an echo from infancy. The music, unaided by any word or programme, told me what Mahler was saying, told me of the scene now being symphonically unfolded at this rehearsal.

The flute blows again, simply and beautifully varied:

The development presses on, ringing changes on short figures taken from the basic thematic and rhythmical material. At once the 'paradise' call assumes impish fantastic shapes:

On hurrying semi-quavers the movement is plainly hurrying somewhere, direction uncertain but intent to push on, never wavering. The sleigh-bells are heard in the minor, without the jingle tone; they suddenly diminish and expand. The movement at this point foretells the subtler 'shadelike' (*schattenhaft*) movement to come later in the Seventh Symphony. Here the atmosphere is not really haunted; the fragments of tune and metre are playful. The rising figure of Ex. 5 (at A) and the first five notes of Ex. 3 and the descending phrase of Ex. 6 (varied), are tossed about, the *tempo* and stresses are unaltered, but not the tonality. The 'sleigh' theme again recurs also transformed:

Perhaps there is too much of this tum-tum-tum-tum. The main melody tries to regain articulation:

17

urged on by the 'paradise' call. The lower wind echoing the cadence of Ex. 9, the instruments jostle through a strenuously composed section, a little mechanical in its rhythmical sequences. A clearance of C major wood-wind and horn recapture the confident Ex. 7.

18

Mahler here gets himself into such a 'kerfuffle' (Kathleen Ferrier's lovely onomatopoeia) that he is obliged to bring to a sudden general pause the whole stampeding orchestra—a *hiatus in manuscriptus*!

19

With a contrivance of felicity, Mahler gets out of this cul-de-sac and opens the way to his recapitulation. He begins, or threatens to begin, all over again, with his first or main theme; or, rather, the fourth and fifth bars of it '*wieder wie im Anfang*':

20

Then he enchantingly goes contrary to our expectations of the theme's continuance by a leap and accent recalling the 'paradise' motif:

and after two bars of

a transition is made quite unashamedly to

and to the dancing Ex. 7, followed by the descent (Ex. 3C) to the broad *Ton!* tune of Ex. 8. But when Mahler recalls a theme in a recapitulation we can at once realise that experience in development has changed it, making it more mature or less naïve. The broad *Ton!* melody is slightly but beautifully altered, with the happiest upward curve of phrase:

Skeleton quotation from the score is here entirely inadquate; the scoring is rich and heartening. Next, 'Mit grossem Ton!' comes Ex. 9, the prim Ex. 9A holding the train, another touch which draws us close to Mahler as ever we can hope to come:

Again the sleigh of the symphony's beginning, now artfully extended until the leaps and descent of

lead to the cadences closing the exposition (Exs. 10, 10A) which are given once more gentle touch of magic and a flavour of Strauss:

Mahler has not finished with his caresses even yet. A horn makes an echo:

28

And now trips in one of the most exquisite little codas in all symphonic music. It has a graciousness which is more moving, in its light-heartedness, if we remember how generally trouble-hearted Mahler was soon to become:

29

The movement happily leaps to its appointed end, thus:

SECOND MOVEMENT

This movement has often been described as a *danse macabre* presumably because the first violin is tuned a tone higher and because in an early sketchbook Mahler wrote the verbal suggestion that here 'Freund Hein spielt auf.' Freund Hein is a legendary fiddler who leads the way to the 'beyond' ('Ein freundlicher Führer zum Jenseits'). He is certainly not depicted in this movement as at all grisly. The many instrumental caprices and oddities—mutes, sharp *pizzicati*, angular melodic and rhythmic figures, unexpected *sforzati* and so on—all these 'effects' contribute to a general impression of humourous grimace. It is *Mahlerisch* 'play'. The movement in fact is transitionary, leading the symphony through a sort of child purgatory, thence along the cloisters of the third and *poco adagio* movement to the paradise of plenty which has always been somewhere ahead of us, though not always in sight.

I

In his next and Fifth Symphony Mahler was to compose his most elaborate Scherzo, a gigantic and, in its Trio, a haunted Scherzo. Such a Scherzo, or even an echo of it, would have ruined the essential 'make believe, once upon a time' mood of the Fourth Symphony. Mahler, whose taste could falter while grappling with the cosmos and all ethical connotations, seldom if ever blemished the style of miniature. His fateful dichotomy was that in him resided the sophisticated and dæmonic and the naïve and heavenly possessed. The second movement of the Fourth Symphony approximates in outward formal show to a Scherzo-Rondo. Really it is aesthetically and musically not much more than a 'round dance' with *Ländler* contrasts. To go happily into the symphonic context the movement simply had to steer clear of those truly demonic and haunted traits of Mahler which later created the Scherzo of the Sixth symphony. 'Freund Hein spielt auf.' The shadows cast momentarily are those of the nursery candlelight. My readers must not suspect from my summary of the symphony's 'content'—child's heaven, gingerbread paradise, sleigh-bells and the rest—that there is mawkishness in the air, hints of Barrie-esque never-never-land embarrassments. Not at all. The work, as a whole, is mature, with fine continuous thinking. Freund Hein and his fiddle disperses whimsy in one phrase, after a horn-call of romance, with a tart answer from *staccati* wind:

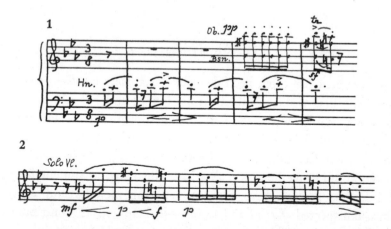

There is something too much of this exchanged among strings and wood-wind, despite touches of phrase by phrase variation. The movement is not, I feel, particularly engrossing in its own right, symphonically or musically; but it prepares the way by its artfully-artless monotony and contrivance for the full-toned Adagio soon to come. And Mahler is again, as in the second movement of the Third Symphony, uncharacteristically brief—again his intuition!

The first contrast—the Trio—is announced by a horn-call:

Now the *Ländler* flavour

continuing

Now a repetition of the Scherzo figuratively changed, with a sharp tang of violins *forte* in the passage:

In this movement Freund Hein, not the devil himself maybe, but no doubt a relation, certainly does not have all the best tunes.

As at the movement's beginning the horn calls, then the Scherzo persists and when the Trio returns there are enchanting variations. The horn sings genially enough

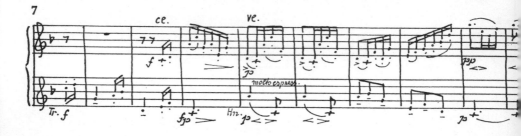

And there are happy touches such as:

and

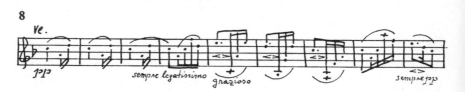

which gives promise of the bliss to come, sooner or later, in the symphony's closing pages, which run to an end this way:

Another glimpse into the heaven's blue, beyond the present landscape, is obtained by a modulation to:

11

It is another antipication of the happy end, for the finale of the heavenly joys begin this way:

12

But keen ears are needed to spot this artful piece of forecasting.

Freund Hein's fiddle now in a reasonably natural tone resumes with less menance than ever and a particularly cheerful variant happens at:

13

the high F now quite a gracious *pizzicato*, not as before, *schwer kurz und gerissen*. Still, the sky dims once more and the harmonies become mildly dissonant, with the horn sounding as mournful as at the movement's beginning. The end is another grimace, playful enough:

14

Of this movement Mahler wrote: 'The Scherzo is mystical, bewildering and weird. But then, in the Adagio, which disentangles everything, you will soon see that, after all, it has not been so bad.' The artist in him kept on the right side of the little angels. There is indeed nothing in the Scherzo

contradicting the main unburdened style of the symphony as a whole—
certainly no tortuously tangled Mahler complexes!

THIRD MOVEMENT

In no other movement in any of his symphonies did Mahler's instinct
for style and fitness lead him in the right direction so well as here.
Obviously a slow movement was now necessary to give substance to the
work as a whole. So far Mahler has been exploring and enjoying a sort
of symphonic playground. And ahead in the fourth and final movement
he is ordained to sing of the heavenly pleasures. A bridge passage was
needed to get there. But an Adagio as large-spanned and intense as the one
ending the third symphony would never have done; it would have enlarged
a wonder world into one of mature contemplation and self-conscious
submission to the sadness and beauty of human-all-too-human existence.

Mahler decided on a Poco Adagio with variations as a *via media*. In a
slow movement not classically elaborate and not too sustainedly devout he
could both play and pray. Some mood of devotion was called for even for
right of entrance to a paradise of fairy and *Wunderkinder*. In this form of an
Adagio with variations, the note of gaiety and blissful anticipation could be
sounded and yet the tone of the movement as a whole could evoke ascent
to an upper ether. Mahler does not put a foot wrong in this Poco Adagio,
perhaps the most unflawed long stretch of music in all his output. Nobody
except Schubert has given us a strain softer, sweeter and more hearteasing
than the movement's beginning, scored only for violas, 'cellos and
contra-basses. It is sheer peace merely to write down this ineffable passage:

1

The *pizzicato*, solemn yet comforting, echoes from the Schubert Quintet.

Violins come in wafted from above, with a 'cello caress underneath later to begin a variation:

Then the oboe mingles this melody with the opening strains:

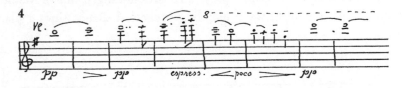

With the double-bass *pizzicato* still softly beating, plucked strings continue, interrupted only by a few sustained notes, for forty bars.

As the oboe plays the melody in Ex. 1 the strings soar in a characteristically high and tense altitude,

the high D held for five bars as the bassoon and horn descend:

And now the violin's high D curves downward and the movement's first and annunciatory period comes to a cadential close, the deep *pizzicato* reluctant to cease:

and there is a lovely aftersong,

pizzicato bass continuing,

until into the symphony comes a strange visitation. Under sustained notes in the wind, the bass fiddles now pluck strings hesitatingly, one of Mahler's 'suspense' figures. Out of the impending orchestral silence sings a plaintive oboe:

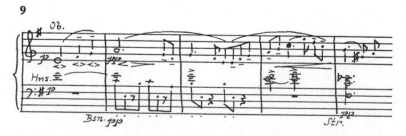

leading to the most *Mahlerisch* of all 'fingerprints'; it steals in beautifully:

This is a strange guest, none other than Mahler himself. So far he has composed more or less objectively, keeping in mind, throughout the first and second movements, both the essential naïvety of the work's basic conception, and also a formal balance in which the whole is on the plane, or leading naturally to the poise of the entirely miniature and unrhetorical finale. Now enters for the first time in all Mahler's symphonies, his theme song, his musical *persona:* let us hear it again, naked:

I take it that the appearance of this theme, so closely verging on a grown-up emotional tension, with something of a self-conscious gesture of yearning in it, signifies one of Mahler's backward glances at the springtime of his life, now going away from him. Again he shows his tact, as he develops the theme; for though the ache and a spiration upwards is continued, there is a flutter of happy decoration:

The theme is immediately varied by:

with a counterpoint from the horn beginning on the sixth bar of the above quotation:

13

And again the Mahler theme climbs up, now burdened with some weight of woe:

14

until a really determined attempt is made at some security of tone and peace of mind:

15

But there is a collapse in a way entirely Mahler's. We have heard much the same sound of orchestral subsidence in the Adagio of the Third Symphony. To the end, in the first movement of the Ninth, following the *Kondukt* passage, we shall hear the same formulae of overthrowal, subtilised of course.

As usual the horn and trumpet signal the descent in this temporary set-back:

16

and the *pizzicato* returns. The movement is now in a condition of suspense. The horn is searching for a new tonality:

From D minor back to G major, then comes one of Mahler's most simply and enchantingly graded variations:

The whole of this variation is gorgeously scored. No composer has endowed lower strings with music surpassing Mahler's. It seems to come from the instrument's mellow wood.

Soon the variation emerges almost imperceptibly into another, gracious and gay:

and the swaying figure, after a lovely turn, becomes shaded. Again the sun is clouded over:

Another strain of melancholy solitariness is heard in an orchestra, which becomes subdued, and as though afraid:

21

Here is an instance of how Mahler, in a few bars,—a bridge passage of the simplest tonal 'joinery'—can pungently denote or expose the introvert side of his personality. From this transitional passage we can *taste* Mahler. The *sound*, the sound alone, is unmistakably Mahler. No other composer has made a sound so absolutely fitting to the marking *klagend*. Though the urgent striving theme tries now quite passionately to assert itself, there is another chromatic fall, saved at the pinch by a curve upward in the lower fiddles, with a key change to complete the consoling harmony, leading to the variation which tells us that the haven is nearing and that the heart of Mahler is as full as it is grateful:

22

Then, this:

23

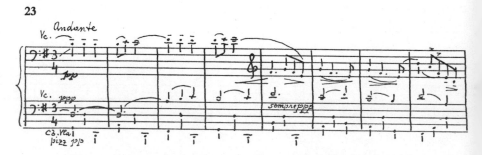

followed by writing of such sumptuousness that it is surely one of the

musicians' experience of mortal bliss to play it. The graciousness begins
to dance lightly,

24

the pace abruptly runs as though ahead of the semi-quavers. The happily
released host, free now of all fears, scampers along threatening the movement's utter disorder. And a horn call solemnly admonishes—in its
context one of Mahler's greatest horn calls, which is saying much.
Magically, we are again in the prayerful atmosphere of the movement's
beginning:

25

But there has been, as always in a Mahler recapitulation, or hint of one,
clarification. A melody comes down from the strings, a laying-on of hands:

26

and, at the last bar of this example, the second violins rise with grace
abounding, surely:

27

But without the orchestration it is frustrating to quote only the thematic outlines.

Horns echo their cadence at the end of the first period of the movement, but now they rise, not fall:

and transcended harmonies are attained:

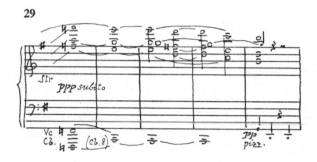

We are back to the movement's first *tempo* and the bass fiddles, with their *pizzicato*, await the return of the Mahler theme but—no, the gates of heaven open in a blaze of arpeggios and harp *glissandi*, as the orchestra modulates in a flash to E major and to the Paradise song, first heard long ago:

and as the portals are wide open comes the calm and the heart's gratitude:

An ascent into the ethereal, *Sehr zart und innig:*

Slowly the strings, with flute and no other instrument, evoke the hush of a region magically above the terrestrial world, and the second violins descend as the movement ends, hovering on a D major half-close (see Ex. 33 on pages 144, 145 and 146 below the line).

FOURTH MOVEMENT

Paradise gained. The clarinet sings a preludial song born of the Paradise motif:

carried on by flute and oboe:

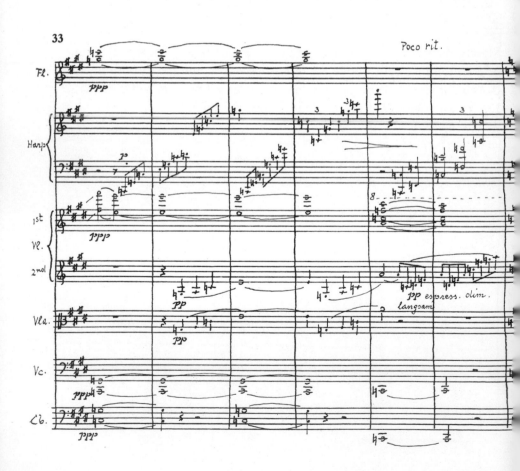

The soprano solo sings and trills of the heavenly enjoyment:

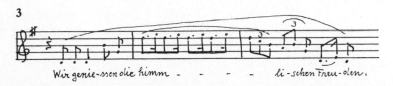

Wir genie-ssen die himm - - - - li-schen Freu-den.

Mahler asks for the utmost discretion in the orchestral accompaniment, and for the absence of any note of parody in the vocalist. She should always avoid the self-conscious and convey an impression of childlike animation, but at the *ritornello* the mood needs, without a 'professional' air of transition, a change to momentary solemnity for 'Saint Peter in heaven looks on':

4

Sanct Pe - ter im Himmel sieht zu !

This is a touch of endearing fancy, archaic parallel octaves and fifths in a context of rippling youthful naïvety. The sleigh figure of the first movement returns three times as the soloist goes her animated way, telling that Saint Luke is killing the oxen and that a lamb also is being led to slaughter. Criticisms have been brought against all this bloodthirstiness in a celestial music never heard on earth. But it is all a dream and we can be sure that the oxen and the lamb survive to take part in the feast. They are merely playing their parts in the ritual. The sounds are heard of the bellowing cattle; and there are the echoes of the cry of the angels in the fifth movement of the Third Symphony, 'Und sollt' ich nicht weinen, Du gütiger Gott'. The racing bells and high jinks break out again, then there is a transformation scene, soft and delectable. Deep tones of the harp, deep plucked strings, a pipe of the pastoral fields, lead us to a Finale not often equalled in symphonic music for gentleness and for a vanishing blissful tone.

5

Kein Mu-sik ist ja ———————— nicht auf Er - den,

E major has been one of the keys of heaven. The end is a lullaby

6

with the harp in rocking motion softer and softer, dominant and tonic of E major.

I have been deliberately naïve in illustrating here the simple notation of Mahler's ending to his Fourth Symphony. He of all composers revelled in a spectacular finish; and eight of his ten completed symphonies (I include under this covering title *Das Lied von der Erde*), end in a violent piling of instrumental accoutrement. Each of the three symphonies to follow the Fourth has a heaven-storming or, if you like, barn-storming Finale. When Mahler visited America and they showed him the Niagara Falls, he listened attentively for a minute then said: 'Endlich fortissimo!' The gentle strains lulling the Fourth Symphony to its cradled close will sound for us all the more lovable (Mahler lovable?!) if we think ahead of the turbulence and the wrath to come, until the tired heart and nerves, but never a tired brain, seek rest in the last movements of *Das Lied* and the Ninth Symphony and the opening Adagio of the Tenth.

In the Fourth Symphony Mahler takes farewell of his youth, and of the *Wunderhorn* world. He has now arrived at a time of great transition, and he has come to the technical mastery which will obey the discipline needed to compose on a large or miniature scale. More important, he has summed up his impressions of adolescence, sung of the first discoveries of life, of heroic aspiration, of the relation of nature and religion to man. He has sung of the flowers, of the beasts of the field, of Kindergarten delights and fears, of the yearnings of early manhood for receding scenes, visions, impulses. He has attained, subjectively, the artist's power to draw experience of life into his own imagination and to shape it in terms of his medium into the world of his will and genius for representation. Henceforth it is Mahler the grown experienced man who will speak, no longer naïve in any of his conceptions. He is, by reason of his hard-won maturity, as man and composer, paradoxically more alone in the world than before. Henceforth he has to face reality: the sounds of the *Wunderhorn* calling him to romantic security and escapism are dying away. Before him is the greater world of personal struggle. He has now to elucidate himself as grown, experienced man and spirit. In the next three symphonies he forges a new and wholly instrumental language. The aid of a consoling traditional poetry is dispensed with, and not until he has 'hammered out' significances entirely in his own language as musician does he, in the Eighth Symphony, turn again for spur to conception to words and poetry inspired from outside his own self and centre. By then he has given full account of himself.

I must correct here any impression I may have given that the Mahler symphonies are *always* a transcription in tone of the thoughts and feeling which possessed him consciously as man reacting to the circumstances of his everyday life. An artist is often conditioned to a large extent, emotionally, imaginatively and as thinking musician, by the experiences he goes through while making his music. To risk a simplification in a complex argument, let me put it this way—he is not obliged to have revelations in the scriptural or strictly religious sense in order to compose a work evoking imaginative reactions hard to distinguish from those conventionally classified as religious. Likewise I, not a Roman Catholic or a believer in any Church's interpretation of what is conveniently called the life spiritual, can be moved deeply by Elgar's *The Dream of Gerontius*.

Mahler was an expressive composer, using his music to clarify and make intelligible to himself all that his antennæ of consciousness reponded to in stimuli from the external universe; but also he was a composer always reacting to prompting from his art as he made it. When he was asked to state his religion he replied, as we have seen, 'I am a musician'. The forces influentially at work on the artist are indeed twofold (at least) and it is hard in abstract reason not to think of them as interrelated. The stimuli from life, from reading, thinking, seeing, enjoying and suffering, and the stimuli from discoveries in his art as he practises it—these factors collaborated, I think, in the creative processes which were Mahler's. In this sense only, and in no factual and ordinary meaning of the word, are his symphonies autobiographical. Of the Fifth Symphony he said (he was referring particularly to the Scherzo but the remarks are true of the work as a whole): 'Die menschliche Stimme würde hier absolut nicht Raum finden. Es bedarf nicht des Wortes, alles ist musikalisch gesagt.' ('Here is absolutely no room for the human voice. Everything is said musically, the word is not needed.')

But Mahler held the opinion that after Beethoven no 'absolute' music had been written at all. In the three instrumental symphonies we come upon another Mahler paradox, or rather, another aspect of his ambivalence, the two contrary sides of his art. The less he depends upon 'the word' the more—certainly not the less!—he makes his tone-symbols pregnant of extra-musical significance. Yet also he presents himself as the 'pure' musician. For example, the Rondo Finales of the Fifth and Seventh symphonies could well be called deliberate essays in virtuoso formalism. The Finale of the Sixth Symphony, in part, is almost academically 'absolute'; it is an instance of Mahler composing inspired, 'Kapellmeister' music. None the less, in the Finale of the Sixth Symphony, hammer blows tell us of the death of the 'hero'. Alma Mahler has testified that in this movement 'the hero receives three hammer blows from fate, the third of which fells him like a tree'. We could infer, without Alma's clue, that the Finale certainly does try to say something 'programmatic'. So with the first movements of each of the 'purely instrumental' Fifth, Sixth and Seventh. In the first notable writings on Mahler by an English music critic, Samuel Langford flashed vivid light: 'In the Fifth Symphony the Faust spirit of the middle-period breaks out with tragic intensity. Its opening march movement, and the march tempo of the Allegro movement of the Sixth, give these symphonies the guise of a pitched battle against the world and the demons of life.' We have only to consider the *stürmisch bewegt* movement of the Fifth to realise and to flavour with joy the felicitous rightness of Langford's phrase, 'pitched battle against the world and the demons of life'. Also Langford refers to Mahler's will to conquer. He has just written of Mahler's occasional emulations of Strauss in his 'melodic weight, swiftness and energy', but then, searchingly he continues, 'Mahler was more serious than Strauss, and his struggle is more openly one of moral temper.' Rivers of ink have gone to writings on Mahler since, in 1920, Langford put down these words, in a press telegram from Amsterdam, at a time when scarcely a note of the instrumental symphonies had been heard in England, and seldom anywhere else. And no Mahlerian since Langford has so aptly summed up Mahler's musical aesthetic, especially as it influenced the composition of the Fifth, Sixth and Seventh symphonies.

Far behind, indeed, are we to travel now from the world of *Wunderhorn*. Mahler is putting childlike things, behind him and as he does so, we can often get a sense of his regrets—and share them.

Symphony No. 5 in C sharp minor

FIVE MOVEMENTS

(1901-02: revisions 1907-09)

THERE WERE PROBABLY reasons not entirely connected with his inner life as artist which impelled Mahler to the composition of symphonic music *per se*. He was vain of his musicianship and hated to be grouped with the 'programme' or illustrative schools. Strauss rather tauntingly described Mahler's music as 'literature'. The joke here is that Strauss, not Mahler, was more or less dependent on 'literature' for musical inspiration. To the end Strauss pondered the relationship, as a fruitful means of interaction, between words and music. His last opera enchantingly plays on the problem—*prima la musica—dopo le parole*. Impossible to separate word and tone, sings Madeleine: 'In eins verschmolzen sind Worte und Töne— zu einem Neuen verbunden.' Such a problem never occurred to Mahler. Words for him simply fertilised music to independent expressive powers.

Fully-armed technically in the prime of his life, aged forty-one, he set to work on the Fifth Symphony in the summer of 1901 at Mayernigg am Wörthersee. One year only came between the finishing of the Fourth and the beginning of the Fifth; but the difference between the two works, the transformation, is tremendous in conception, bulk, weight, and extension of the means of communication. With a mastery of the orchestral language unequalled by any composer of his period, by few since (excepting those who have learned from him by emulation), he could now give instinctive play to music-making as symphonist. If deep down in him *das Wort* had any guiding force on his musical conceptions, he needed no direct sign or influence from extra-musical sources of conception. His tone symbols had by this time taken into their own texture, their own being, melodic, rhythmical, chordal or colouristic, every association inviting verbal definition. At the beginning of the Fifth Symphony, for example, the Mahlerian fanfare, first blown on the winds of youthful romantic fancy, has become a sinister trumpet call of fate sounding in a nature-haunted imagination. It is true that in this symphony, as in the

Seventh, echoes from songs of Mahler are heard. But quotations from them are merely incidental, not thematically productive, nor in any way influencing the symphonic argument. The *Wunderhorn* songs, as we have seen, very importantly conditioned a whole symphonic shape or sequence. In the first movement of the Fifth, Mahler brings in, note for note, a measure from the first of the *Kindertotenlieder.* The Adagietto, as again we have seen, grows from the Rückert setting, 'Ich bin der Welt abhanden gekommen.' But I have already pointed out that the shape and tone-symbol of 'Ich bin der Welt abhanden gekommen' has been anticipated in the Poco Adagio of the Fourth Symphony, and is, in fact, a Mahler fingerprint of life-long power of identity. Quotations from the Rückert settings, which were composed, or were in some condition of germination while Mahler was also becoming pregnant with the Fifth Symphony, do no more than illumine the general mood of the composer as, by instrumental weapons alone, he girds himself to action.

Symphonie für grosses Orchester was Mahler's title. And he scored it for four flutes, piccolo, three oboes, cor anglais, three clarinets, bass clarinet, three bassoons, contra-bassoon, six horns, four trumpets, three trombones, tuba, timpani, side-drum, bass-drum, cymbals, triangle, Glockenspiel, tam-tam, harp and strings. Alma Mahler, whom Mahler married shortly after the Fifth was finished, tells in her book (*Gustav Mahler: Erinnerungen und Briefe*) of the first rehearsal—'Mahler had overscored the percussion instruments and kettle-drums so madly and persistently that little beyond the rhythm was recognisable.' 'You've written it for percussion and nothing else,' she said. Mahler was revising the score almost until the month of his death. Seven years after the first performance of the Fifth, Mahler wrote of the instrumentation: 'I fail to comprehend how I could then have blundered as like a novice.' He could never leave things alone; he was driven to self-criticism and self-correction not only because he was a perfectionist; but also because he never felt secure as man or artist. His visions blinded him. Towards his life's end he was humbly blaming his activities in opera as a cause of faults and 'impurities' in his symphonies—if only he had been able earlier in his career to sink his mind entirely in symphonic music!

In fact, the Fifth symphony as a whole is composed with much firmness, with a far-seeing grip on the structure, with a rare understanding of instrumental individuality and textural balance. The Adagietto is for strings and harp alone, an essay in the use of the chamber orchestra. The foaming, roaring, raging sea of sound is often uncompromising in its thematic independence, despite a quite fiercely polyphonic motive power. In the Rondo Finale we even catch a glimpse of Mahler the Kapellmeister.

Enjoying a freedom from the metrical shapes necessary in quasi-Lied composition, Mahler now elaborates his expositions. The Fifth Symphony, after a trumpet fanfare, embarks on a long funeral march, which is contrasted with a strenuous section of quite reckless agitation: *Plötzlich schneller, leidenschaftlich. Wild.* Phrases in these sections are removed from one context, transformed and then put with absolute relevance into another context. The second movement is related by a hard-won signal of triumph to the even more hardly won victory of the symphony's last pages. And the second movement is really a development or extension of the first. The fourth movement, the Adagietto, is linked thematically to the fifth and final movement. The centre piece of the whole is the Scherzo, which is a *Ländler* Waltz in apotheosis. We have seen Mahler's efforts in the First, Second and Fourth symphonies to give connection to movements by means of thematic and rhythmical cross-references. In the Fifth the integration is achieved by methods which go deeper conceptually and call for a larger and a yet more searching bird's-eye view. In other words, the large sky of the Fifth, and of all the subsequent Mahler symphonies, is encompassed without losing sight of subsidiary detail. Not a sparrow of a crotchet falls unheeded; though the detail may, again, not be musically impressive at first sight or hearing, the organisation of it into a tonal whole psychologically as well as symphonically is arresting—here surely is a *Mahlerisch* achievement which is clearly demonstrable. It is a strange notion, still current amongst music critics and Bachelors of Music, that Mahler was a composer of song-symphonies without ability to build largely and consecutively. Nonsense.

He rings the changes on small phrases with dramatic and musical aptness, making cross references sometimes easy to miss in performances, sometimes easy to make too much of. But thematic transformations are only one way of musical re-creation or procreation; and, perhaps, for the uses of music which seeks to probe human consciousness, not the most searching, since strict thematic transformation tends to remain a matter of rearrangement of surface sound. Mahler develops and integrates frequently by rhythmical changes, pertinence of instrumental commentary, the instruments making unexpected entrances with themes last heard played in a different context by another and entirely different instrument. As an example of Mahler's genius for using an orchestra as dramatis personæ, consider the foreboding trumpet motif beginning the Fifth Symphony and its spectral attentuated echo at the first movement's close.

In the Fifth's first movement the opening funeral march is immediately assaulted, as though protest is being hurled at its elegiac resignation. The violins are let loose:

1(A)

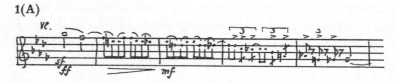

A rebellious trumpet trumpets:

2

and the racing strings get a more clinching grip on the stormy height:

3

This vehement protest is actually drawn into a variant of the funeral march in the second movement, and treads the way (with Mahler) of submissive woe. Like this:

4

trailing its robe of woe slowly onwards.

The famous Adagietto

is parodied into banality in the Rondo Finale

Mahler marked this lilting, mocking, pretty piece of mimicry, *Zart, aber ausdrucksvoll*—also *grazioso*. I can only think he was here being funny. I give him the benefit of the doubt. Heard for the first time, with the Adagietto still lingering in mind, this variation comes rather as a shock. Then, in the fresh context, we begin to see the joke. Mahler could turn an ironic whip on himself.

I refer to these changes of figure not merely to emphasise Mahler's cleverness at tonal *legerdemain*; in any case, as thematic transformations pure and simple, these are not necessarily convincing. But I hope I am showing the *ironic* interest, to say the least, in Mahler's way of bringing a theme disguised only sufficiently to suggest a mask of mockery, into a context which surely makes for irony.

FIRST MOVEMENT

The first movement of the Fifth Symphony is not, of course, Mahler's first extended essay in a large-scaled funeral march, large enough, that is, to maintain a large symphonic shape. The first movement of the Second Symphony could answer to this description. (I don't bring into this category the funeral march of the Second Symphony; it is an interlude and not a symphonic first movement, anyhow.) But the funeral march of the Second Symphony is dramatically presented; the young imagination of the composer takes active part, with its immediate graveyard descents and shudders. Mahler now laments in a slow-moving submissive cortège. First, there is a bodeful summon for trumpet, all other instruments silent until the climax at A:

8

With the triplet throb of the orchestra now accompanying, the coffin is buried, the horns dropping the clods of earth:

9

We have moved from C-sharp minor to G-sharp minor already. The funeral march, the funeral lamentation, has a deliberate monotony. Its inimitable forerunner, I think, is the funeral march in the Chopin Piano Sonata

10

After twenty bars of numbed motion, the fanfare sounds again, this time attempting a more defiant cadence. Consolation lifts up the funeral march at its continuation, the 'cellos indulging Mahler's favourite ornament:

Wood-wind and violas bear up as bravely as well they can, in the circumstances:

B)

Even a gleam of sunshine falls on the obsequies:

3

Only for a moment. The long exposition suspires in a throb of the drum. The themes of the march are not developed in the subsequent section, which begins with the attack of whirling strings (marked 1A, p. 154 above, and by Mahler marked *Plötzlich schneller. Leidenschaftlich. Wild.*) When first I heard this section it struck me as so much nervous excitement, sound and fury. In fact, this contrast of tempo, dynamic and motif to the general burden of the funeral march is absolutely concentrated and balanced to a bar. The trumpet rides above the racing fiddles:

14

and

15

As I have said, Mahler's material is not consistently first-class or thematically memorable—in his '*Wild*' passages especially—but the control, yes the economy, is masterly.

The recurrent fanfare keeps us to the movement's main argument and character. The horn is also prophetic of the great elegy of the second movement,

16

At the crescendo there is a horn figure and flourish which tells us that Mahler had his very natural moments of envy of Strauss:

17

This *plötzlich schneller* section, like the funeral march section, has its own material, which is developed independently—that is, without reference to the content of the other section, except for the binding trumpet fanfare, which Mahler always brings in with musical and dramatic aptness as a sort of recurrent coda. The decrescendo—*allmählich sich beruhigend*—has a shudder in the 'basses; and again the trumpet is imperative; also we hear the opening sinister signal:

18

The funeral march, as though oblivious of the violent storms that have blown, returns stoically in the recapitulation, the wind bearing the

changed re-modulated melodies, the string silent, except for a few sub-sidiary viola bars (solo), until the pendant (Ex. 12B, p. 157) is reached. At the cadential end Mahler makes his *Kindertotenlieder* reference:

19

'Heil, sei dem Freudenlicht der Welt.' Not yet, though, is Mahler in his Fifth Symphony to see the light. Over the dolorous triplet figure (from the *Leidenschaft* fanfare) the violins softly commune in A minor:

20

The honourable Bekker calls this a new idea: 'Leitet zu einem neuen Gedanken von ausdrucksvoll erhabener Prägung.' But it is really the beginning of the *plötzlich schneller, leidenschaftlich* brass motives, (Exs. 2 and 14 above) now presented in highly imaginative augmented varia-tion. The militant Straussian motif rises, with the violins making a con-trary motion more Straussian still:

21

In a tense chromatic descent of sustained notes, the trumpet fanfare is once more assertive; then, by a sudden simple but bodeful change of harmony, anticipating a similar descent in the third and Scherzo movement, mists enshroud the orchestra:

The strings go down to the deep, over the first trumpet-signal with solemn falling changing sustained harmony. And the trumpet's

is faintly echoed on high by the flute. A single *pizzicato* bass note silences the movement, which obviously is not an end. The second movement is, we feel, at hand, ready to explode into further contention.

SECOND MOVEMENT

Marked *stürmisch bewegt* to begin with, *Mit grösster Vehemenz*, 'cellos, basses and bassoons:

Flutes, oboes and clarinet cry out panic-stricken

2

The movement is not only pendant to the first; it is very much a fantasia on themes from the first, yet in itself is a masterly essay in sonata form. We have already made note of one or two germ-cells. The leaping ninth interval, hinted, in the violas, to quick ears or quick eyes during the *Trauermarsch*, is a principal mourner throughout the beautifully-phrased and modulated *molto cantando* procession going its way after the stormy prelude has momentarily subsided.

3

Bekker calls this theme 'die leisen Schmerzenslaute'; it appears, actually or by suggestion, time after time in nearly every instrumental part. As we have remarked above, it now reappears at the eruption of the second movement, angrily distorted from the plumed pathetic motion nodding in the cortège music. In the *Trauermarsch* of the first movement, let us remind ourselves, this motif of a ninth, was heard in the *molto expressive* variation:

4

The other importantly fruitful germ themes in the first movement

5

and

6

are, to use Ernest Newman's much loved phrase, 'definitely seminal', as we shall see at once and hereafter. In this movement especially we are able to consider at its most inventive Mahler's capacity for turning tune fragments to imposing purposes. The attack on the movement is head-long. The violins tear up and down:

7

But there is a firm controlling pivot of steely chords which appear again at the dying down of the tumult, thus pillaring the storm-tossed prelude.

8

At a first hearing of this *stürmisch bewegt* section those listeners who are not initiated Mahlerians might well become allergic to him for ever. At a first sounding, here is orchestral confusion headlong and rhetorical, conductor's formulae, gathered right and left. I have known good musicians compare the section unfavourably with the *allegro non troppo* of the first movement of Tschaikovsky's *Pathétique*; and I have seen their point—as far as a demonstration of similarity of orchestral procedure is concerned. But there was nothing, absolutely nothing, in common between Mahler and Tschaikovsky, as men or composers, except that each naturally took advantage of the instrumental stock-in-trade of expressive symbols in current coin in their heyday.

To the sound of defiant fanfare triplets in horn, trumpet and wind, violins race onward to a downhill, to a dominant, cliff-edge, then the lower strings surge menacingly in A minor:

9

The *schmerz* figure clings to the urgent subterranean propulsion—(but seldom do we hear it in an actual performance of the passage I have just quoted). Despite the emphasis, the nervous assertiveness of this section, the scoring is extraordinarily clean, with no superfluous flesh. Mahler is developing his own athletic linear texture, rare in the symphonic composition of his period. The themes are entirely motoristic, if I may invent the term; they are urgent, dynamic factors of texture, not particularly individual in a strictly musical sense. The strings are taut and springy:

10(F)

I mark this figure F for future reference.

There are recurrent fanfares, almost needless to say:

11

The staccato chords beat again. A typical Mahler descent of wood-wind, and the violas and first violins are left suddenly isolated with

12

The orchestra is in a heartbeat of expectancy:

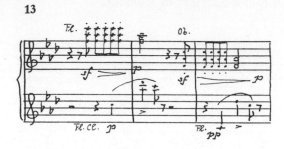

Here comes one of Mahler's most fulsome melodies (he was, by the way, a very natural and prolific melodist!), *Bedeutend langsamer*—in the tempo of the first movement's *Trauermarsch*, of which it is of course a variant in music form of the *Schmerzenslaut*, the pain or sorrow motif, now consoling and appealing.

continuing

From the violins rises an elegy. In my analysis of the first movement I have shown how it is born of an apparently insignificant, certainly not an elegiac figure, for the horn:

The interchange of phrases between violins, violas and 'cellos is extremely beautiful. And all the time wind and horns and trombones persist with the *Trauermarsch* tread; and the *Schmerzenslaut* is ubiquitous.

'Without expression' the flutes and 'cellos take another turn:

17

The Mahler tension comes again, straining upwards:

18

A sudden *Mahlerisch* nervous 'tic' following a diminished seventh chord

19

and the old menace is heard

20

The course of the movement is now challenged by another fanfare variant, strangely enough not from the brass but from violins and wood-wind:

21

The brass menance and the stabbing chords remain obstinate, so trumpets ride into battle

The violins and trombones also bring up reinforcements:

But there is (again and again in Mahler) an unexpected running down of the orchestral motor power. A flurry of quavers, then a caesura. Often in Mahler the transition is achieved less by a truly symphonic change of tonality than by a peremptory halt, as though Mahler were out of inspirational breath. He begins again—yet in the end the 'joins' seem thoroughly well carpentered into a logically shaped whole. Mahler turns on himself reflectively. The orchestra becomes silent and passive, except for the 'cellos and violas. The 'cellos intone recitative lamenting the departed F minor song of consolation; here is a recitative which is really implicit melody, warm, eloquent, lonely, echoing the movement's *Schmerz* tone:

A drum-roll murmurs, and not until the eighteenth bar do the violas enter. It is, in its context, one of Mahler's most moving passages, revealing

the softer, sweeter part of him, the true poet of melancholy, not always the heaven-stormer or the keen brained far-seer, attractive to the young and rebellious of his admirers.

The elegiac melody comes in again in E-flat minor from the horns. What we have probably thought of as an exclusively grateful string song sounds entirely native to the horn; such was Mahler's understanding of the varied expressive scope of any instrument.

25

It goes on until the strings as before aspire upwards in Mahler's habitual semi-tone sequences,

26

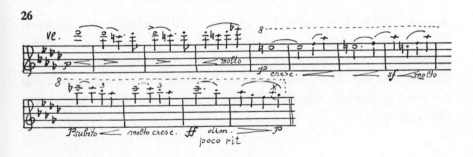

with another abrupt turn:

27

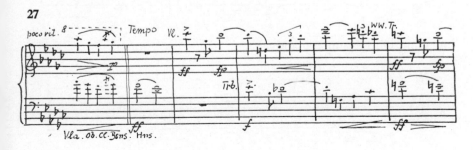

It is one of Mahler's 'popular' tunes, here signifying an escape from emotional tension. A horn supports the effort at cheerfulness:

28

The *Schmerz* figure, reduced to a seventh, brings in phrases from the *Trauermarsch* of the first movement, to the rhythm of the recently discovered hopeful jauntiness. As it dies down there is another effort at confident assertion.

29

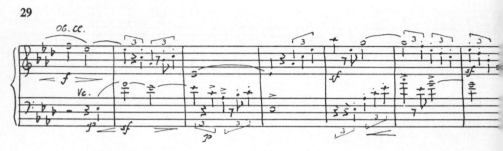

A weak affair in shape and metre, it is doomed to struggle hard to survive. The staccato chords come again impotently. An A major urge at victory merely adds to the orchestral strenuousness. A reckless chromatic landslide leads to the old menace, now in E minor; but pulling himself and his score masterfully together, Mahler resorts to the elegiac theme and the G string:

30

mingling with example F above:

31

The drive onward is free and forceful; a definable end is imminent. We hear again the trumpet's signal:

32

But yet another effort and great push are needed. Violins strain higher, only to collapse once more. Then comes the Herculean thrust:

33

Repeated, shuddering thrusts:

34

A last desperate heave, octave above—and D major is achieved. A chorale?

No mastery, no consummation even now. A fanfare expresses defiance, rather than victory:

36

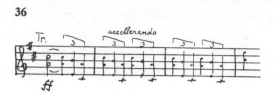

and at last, *fff*, the dawn on the summit—in D major. We have travelled as far as that from the symphony's beginning in C-sharp minor:

37

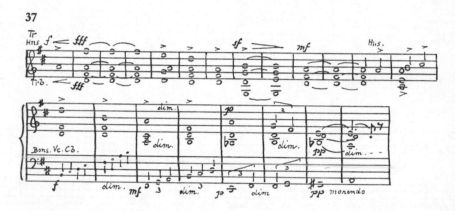

The cadence softens. The mood is suddenly solemn. Not yet the goal and the release. In any case, inner psychological states and developments of soul in search of a sovereign end notwithstanding, Mahler is composing a symphony, and there are other movements to come. Clearly as musician he was obliged to hold back complete tonal consummation. Here he finds a mountain-height which reveals the distant and desirable peak. This chorale crowns the Rondo Finale of the symphony. Now the hurly-burly sets in yet again. Chromatic and rapid subsidences; and the stamping staccato figure is increased in notes and emphasis. With one of Mahler's abrupt and arbitrary transitions the atmosphere changes remarkably. Harps in the air. A coda of twanging instruments, mysterious. A solo violin whispers the *Schmerz* motif. A thunder crack of the drum makes an end. Mahler asks for some rest, some surcease. *Folgt lange Pause.* No wonder. The two complementary opening movements of the Fifth

Symphony may be thought of as one act. The elaborate Scherzo which comes next, is an act in itself. The Adagietto and the Rondo Finale make a third and balancing summing-up in which Mahler as man and musician emerges all the stronger, if not any more integrated, for the ordeal he has gone through. He has worked harder in the Fifth Symphony than ever before. Think of the-sure-of-himself Richard Strauss!

The chorale heard in the second movement of the Fifth has been likened to a Bruckner chorale; indeed, critics have suggested that Mahler here owes a debt to Bruckner for guiding if not inspirational influence. But a Bruckner chorale tells us, as I say, of the abounding grace fallen on him. A Bruckner chorale is a sturdy hymn of faith. Mahler, in this chorale, both as it is heard in the movement we have been considering, and as we shall hear it in the Rondo Finale, is not announcing spiritual assurance. He is trying to convince himself that he can somehow find it by power of his will. Bruno Walter has written 'No spiritual experience, however hardly won, was ever his secure possession.' Even as a composer rich in the materials of his art, a master of it with complete command over the tone symbols he needed to say his say, he was always in danger of over-emphasis, too much elaboration of the part at risk of disturbing the whole and the poise of style. He could not leave well alone; he is seldom reticent. As we have seen, he seldom relaxes throughout a slow movement; the tension returns. The Adagietto in this Fifth Symphony is pathetic because momentarily his dæmon is exhausted. He was religious without sure faith, a prophet without a creed. Also he was a master composer who often found music an inadequate means of self-expression and self-realisation. An artist's 'works' were for him 'the ephemeral and mortal part of him; but what a man makes of himself—what he becomes through the untiring effort to live and to be, is permanent'.[1] In the Fifth, Sixth and Seventh symphonies he is going along the Faustian way to the realms, above the battle, of the Eighth and Ninth and *Das Lied von der Erde*. And in the end he could at long last cry out, 'Verweile doch, du bist so schön'.

THIRD MOVEMENT

The third movement has been written about solemnly and portentously. Mahler himself described it this way:[1] 'The Scherzo is—the very

----

[1] Letter to Alma Mahler, 27 June 1909.

devil. . . . Conductors for the next fifty years will take it too fast and make nonsense of it—and the public? Heavens, what are they to make of this chaos of which new worlds are for ever being created, only to crumble into ruins the moment after. What are they to say of these dancing stars, of this primeval music?' There is, as we have heard, 'primeval' music at the beginning of the Third Symphony. But here most of the tunes and rhythms are irresponsibly gay (for Mahler) *Ländler* melodies and rhythms banalised with tremendous gusto. Donald Mitchell has acutely noted how Mahler absorbed the *Ländler* into the Viennese waltz—alluring in a sophisticated ball-room way. 'Mahler in a sense', writes Mr Mitchell, 'murdered the *Ländler*, but in so doing lent it new life.' Mahler didn't 'murder' the *Ländler*; he ravished it and got it with child—a lusty irreverent waltz rhythm, quick of brain and nerve. The Scherzo of this symphony (in the long run!) is tremendously dynamic and sentimental by turn, redolent not of the *Heimat* but of the glittering city. We can understand Mahler's view of the Scherzo; he was always likely to use portentous language to describe his own music. The original conception or vision obsessed him probably to the extent of making him more or less incapable of hearing a composition of his own objectively—at least not until he had heard several performances of it. His critics, not being involved in the creative process, might surely be able to give a truer account of the Scherzo's style and significances. Edward Perry, on the cover of a record, goes so far as to maintain that its 'searing irony' is prophetic of the twilight of the Austro-Hungarian dynasty!

As a fact, the Scherzo is entirely free of Mahlerian introspection and tension. Here is a substantial example of Mahler the composer, engrossed in his tone-world as artist, momentarily escaped from his psychological dæmon, intent on shapes and patterns, masterfully moulding them, tossing them gigantically about, inventing and transforming to the extent of eight-hundred bars, all in three-four time, revelling in his resources, cocking a snook at traditional music-lore, content for a while with composition, pure and simple or, rather, not so simple: how did it happen that Mahler, great artificer of this movement, ever came to be called naïve? The Scherzo is profuse in musical sophistications; Mahler changes the character of the *Ländler* by taking it out of the fresh air and rooting it in his own civilised cosmopolitan and orchestral habitat; he gives to it a self-conscious inviting poise. For example:

1

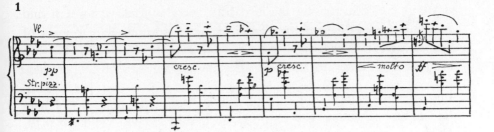

The movement begins with a swagger and flourish by four horns:

2

and a solo horn, who soon is to have the time of his life, gets the dance vigorously on to the floor:

3

The uninhibited lilt is not likely to awaken the momentarily dozing dæmon in Mahler. Contrary to all expectations (or apprehensions) aroused by customary descriptions of this Scherzo ('terrific'—Paul Stefan; 'colossal'—Redlich), the movement goes its way, half café-music, half *Ländler*, Mahlerised.

These themes prance or tiptoe on the heels of the opening galumphing horn:

4

The horns continue their opening figure, varied—of course; then for some dozen bars the fiddles parody the dance with a show of sourness

5

but a gentle sequence of rippling thirds from flutes and bass–clarinet lead to an enchanting, and too brief spell of tip-toeing, Mahler 'out of' Delibes (to use the racing stable's language), Glockenspiel thrown in:

6

Mahler now exploits a bridge-passage, one of his habitual marking-time figures, which though thematically a reach-me-down device, yet has vitality, because it is charged with a certain motor exuberance. Even here there is variation. Often a phrase of melody or a short rhythmical pulsation is a connecting link in the Mahler thinking process.

7

Now the themes are fugally tossed about and a phrase of the main dance returns, tonally diversified; then Mahler adds yet another waltz tune, syncopated in the wood-wind:

8

Already we have heard, in a hundred bars or so of the movement's prodigal exposition, more than half-a-dozen dance tunes racy enough to set up an operetta for life. An effort is made by the horn and trumpet to recall the opening invitation to the dance (Ex. 2) but with a change of key and a sudden variation from *ff* to *pp*, Mahler veils the happy scene with

D major to B major; and with *pizzicato* allurements, the violins languish in *glissando Schmalz* made piquant:

This coy visitant is gorgeously raped in the movement's Finale. The 'cellos curl upward:

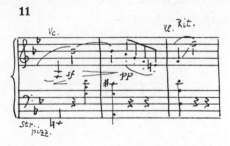

and the oboe whispers the amours of the salon—*Zart*:

After a brief recapitulation of the horn-call and dance, the call now announced by the trumpet, wild stamping begins in the violins again, spreading by imitation through all the strings. Trumpet and horn call and respond in an isolated phrase, soon to have prominence as a romantic signal:

In a sudden calming *legato*, the horn, *portamento* and melancholic, calls from a distance

Wood-wind echo the strain, and now the horn seems to remember, tries again to dominate, but suffers unexpected frustration as the oboes outline a theme by which the instrument will become magically transformed. An insistent straining of the figure

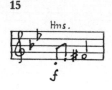

and the orchestra becomes empty, dark, with the big drum booming the Mahler spectral perspective. Now the scene and atmosphere are mysteriously sounding with echoes of

The great solemnity which visits the scherzo of Schubert's C-major Quintet is here echoed

ending in a haunting horn cadence. *Pizzicato* imitations of the solo horn are stealthily plucked as the calls and responses momentarily cease, and the oboe wanly suggests the earlier dance:

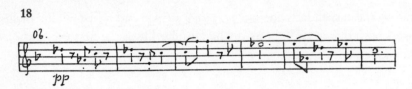

For nearly a hundred bars Mahler makes a fantasy, of

changing tone by having it played on different instruments. We have already, in the first movement of the Third Symphony, heard what he could do with fanfares. Here the *Stimmung* is different. Here is not *leblose Natur* but a haunted landscape, spectral with history and old tales. And here, at last, the Scherzo loses its earlier lightheartedness. Here at last is music which was bound to startle listeners half a century ago, listeners classically brought up. For these calls and echoes are at one and the same time alluring and inimical, and they hold up the movement rather too long. Mahler could never leave our imagination merely kindled; he had to fan it to flame upon flame. The echoes die down beautifully:

M

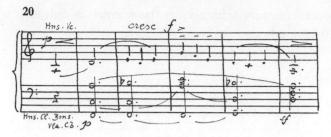

and the *obbligato* horn follows with

and on the suspended cadence, *pizzicato* strings and a first-violin melody
dispel both dream and ghosts by the familiar lilt of the first trio-section of
the movement:

Waltz indeed rapes *Ländler*. It swirls; it savages the three-four time. The
movement is reckless, yet masterfully controlled. It is not dæmonic but
abandoned, rebellious, exultant. Mahler can never have enjoyed himself
so much as here. The general flavour and sound, as well as the tempo, are
prophetic of Ravel's *La Valse*.

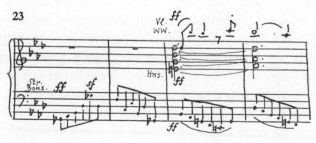

A rattle—*Holzklapper*—beats out an unashamed rhythm:

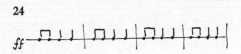

Without a hiatus or obviously contrived change of gear, the recapitulation begins with the opening horn signal and the other attendant motifs. But there is not a hint of automatic repetition. The themes reappear without the air, shape or lilt, of themes which have been developed to the full and are no longer capable of further exploration. Each returns as though by its own free will, as in an exposition, eager for new adventure, with one exception which I leave to the ingenuity of my readers to seek out.

So free of will are they, that so far from being given a conventional recapitulation we are again well in the fray and heart of controversy, lusty argument, phrase challenging phrase, tone set against tone; and all the time the three-four pulse beats healthily as ever. And at the *crescendo* of pace and sound of the recapitulation there is a completely unexpected silence as the horn, again solemnly solo, intones

And in a pulsating orchestra the call and echoes go on, blown on the wind, quite magically modulated and transformed, either in cadence or by context:

and

27

Finally:

28

A headlong coda, neck to neck every player, the contention and gusto terrific and exhilarating, with the rape of the motif aforesaid.

29

The fury is again calmed with the melancholy cadential echoes of the horn which are amongst the most beautifully evocative of any written for the instrument. And the call of horn, which set the movement into action, has the last word in a typical Mahler knock-out. The student will enjoy himself seeking to point exactly where one trio of the movement ends and the other begins, so cunningly integrated is each part in the whole, a synthesis of *Ländler*, Waltz and rondo elements.

FOURTH AND FIFTH MOVEMENTS

The Adagietto has for years been heard by audiences who have not known a note of the rest of the symphony. It has often been taken out of its context and played as a solo piece in a concert programme. And there it has most times been sweetened to drooling sentimentality by excessive string *portamenti*. Heard in its proper place, it comes as an island in stormy season—a point of rest. It contains only some hundred bars; Mahler, composer of the longest movements in symphonic literature, is in the Adagietto, communing with himself and, what is more, revealing the essential Mahler. He is here content to make music with strings and harp alone. The opening phrase, as I have already pointed out, is one of Mahler's most readily recognised fingerprints. Also it is a near relation to the Rückert settings: 'Ich bin der Welt abhanden gekommen' and 'Nun seh' ich wohl'.

The Adagietto is not really a movement in itself. It's too much of a *Lied* to serve as a full-scale movement. At the dying fall of an unresolved cadence at the Adagietto's end—Mahler asks for the pause then—*attaca Rondo Finale.*

This Adagietto is original in its melodic shaping:

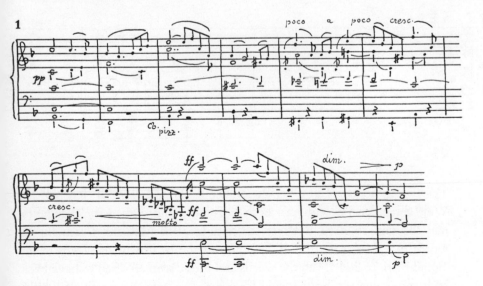

The middle section suddenly disturbs the musing cadences of the opening

phrases; here is the Mahler ache, if ever, not of pain but of some happiness
or peace not entirely found and taken:

The movement dies down in a twilight of harp *arpeggio*, the strings in
emphatic submission, unresolved but hopeful—the triumphant Finale is
round the corner:

The falling notes are as a variant on the orchestral close of 'Ich bin der
Welt abhanden gekommen'; both beginning and end of the Adagietto
may be said to have Rückert associations. But Mahler's treatment of
words in a *Lied* is entirely different from the treatment of words in his
Wunderhorn period. Then the words and music seemed often to have been
each spontaneously born joined together. It is a characteristic of a folksong that words and tune are inseparable—which came first, the egg or the

hen? By the time Mahler set Rückert to music he had developed into the very jealous musician, always on guard lest he should be labelled as a composer dependent for inspiration and ability to shape a work on a 'programme'. Mahler was a vain man as far as his own music was concerned. I am pretty sure that he wrote his three instrumental symphonies partly from a determination to prove himself as musician first and foremost. The settings of the Rückert songs have a more subtle and musical inflection and transition than we can find in the *Wunderhorn* series; his melody is more conscious of its turns, of its chromatic points of emphasis. And the harmony is less homophonic. The Rückert songs in short, are musically germinated. In plainer words, Mahler the musician has by chance found words needed by his musical pregnancy. In the *Wunderhorn* songs, the words, not the music, were the tone-bearers, the tone-inspirers.

His Fifth Symphony is Mahler's most musically self-contained work (despite the so-called Rückert cross-references). In the Rondo Finale, especially, he put forth all his tonal resources, all his manifold craftsmanship as composer, in a movement which is as a horn of plenty, fruitful and brimming over with all the musician's devices, classic and modern— polyphony rapid and moving as though on velvet in fugal double harness, with the rondo sections in contrast flux and metamorphosis. To quote in print the main themes will not be altogether enlightening. Here is music, organised tone patterns, with nothing to discuss or fulfil but itself. The movement is Mahler's most 'absolute'; he tried again in the finale of the Seventh Symphony, to subdue his hand to the substance that it worked in—but vainly and more or less repetitively.

This Rondo Finale begins with a summons for the first horn. It is not one of Mahler's menacing fanfares, but a genial call, sustained and *verklingend*. It is echoed by the violins. Then another horn call, simple tonic and dominant, which is humorously answered by the bassoon, with an echo of a phrase from the Mahler song: 'Lob des hohen Verstandes.' It is one of the richest examples of irony to be found in all music; for with a scholarly movement getting under way, fugues, double-fugues and what not in readiness for action, Mahler's quotation refers to the song's theme: argumentative contest between cuckoo and nightingale, the ass as judge. Nowhere else is Mahler so much the free inexhaustible musician as now:

1

Horn, clarinet and bassoon hold conference, obviously planning the course of action in the festivities soon to begin.

Another horn-call, more animated, is hesitatingly answered by the clarinet:

2

In twenty bars is contained all the movement's germinal themes. And now, *allegro giocoso*, the movement glides down the stocks into open sea:

3

The sonority and breadth of the music, here especially, is of a warm *gemütlich* kind not often heard in Mahler. It is almost German (or Brahmsian) in its amplitude and contentment. And ideas breed ideas. The first fugue comes in on a rhythmic suggestion of the chorale of the second movement's Finale:

4

The strings have so far been silent, except the 'cellos, who introduce the fugue:

This sequence of notes is active more or less throughout the movement. Mahler's counterpoint, usually bony and far from cosily *Kapellmeisterisch*, is for the moment (until the advent of the Sixth Symphony!) high spirited and elastic. Moreover, it is not in its parts so starkly individual that it cannot submit to blended harmony succulently rooted. Mahler's polyphony does not insist on strict vertical listening; there is usually combined with the linear interest a 'pull' of fundamental harmony, even it if is only a pedal.

With Mahler's running quasi-fugal figure he combines mainly two others, to begin with, the refrain from the chorale of the second movement, and the echo of the '*Lob des hohen Verstandes*':

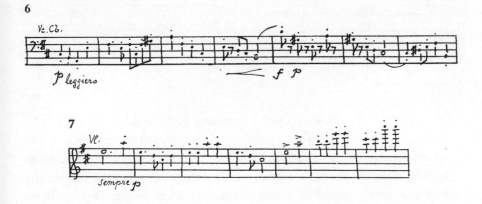

The movement proliferates phrase by phrase. We shall hear much of

This motif is of course germinated by the first three bars of the movement. Incidental figures glide into the constant movement on and on:

which is immediately used as a counterpoint to:

The return of the *Giocosa*, deep toned and gorgeously scored, leads to the rapid quavers of the fugue; and now we come to the humour of the transformation of the Adagietto theme. It is introduced by a march-rhythm of much pomp, the ubiquitous interval of a fourth the leader, scurrying along too, like urchins running after—with, and in front of, a procession. This is now propelled forward by a swagger in the horns:

Then the strings—*grazioso*—unashamed:

To a full hearted cadence the changed melody ends, with curious bell harmonies in the strings, the ding-dong of Ariel, a strange visitation to such company:

The movement makes brief fantasy on the Adagietto theme until the fugue interrupts the reverie. The march motion comes again and the chorale theme is secularised. It has never been Brucknerian in solemnity.

Nicht eilen, Martello, Staccatissimo, Strich für Strich—these cautionary signs come one upon the other. The fugue takes charge of the entire orchestra, six horns and two trumpets blare out martial fanfares

15

and

16

The pace does not slacken and the entire orchestra is alive and propulsive. Another reinforcement to the perpetual motion elbows its way unceremoniously in:

17

Horns and trumpets march with this theme, modifying the oboe figure of the seventh bar of the introduction to the movement. The movement, indeed, is a rondo plus—theme after theme returning with fresh identity. If they are not always charged in rotation they seem to have acquired a new and creative musical purpose by appearing in another context, rhythmical or by shaping a different texture which, none the less, remains always true to the main character of the movement. I am aware that my quotations convey as sketchy an impression of this wonderful Finale as if I were showing you a broad outlined map of a teeming fruitful landscape, expecting you to receive from it a comprehensive view of its abounding, abundant life. The first three notes of the Adagietto parody are mingled in a neck-and-neck race of a double-fugue. A climax is achieved; then the Adagietto motif shakes itself free of development fetters and, enjoying individual liberty again, goes to the cadence of its first appearance in the Finale. 'Ding dong' once more; and the march continues, the fugue setting pace and direction. Mahler's favourite heaving or swinging leverage—at this period in his music—promises a decisive peroration. The fugue is shared by the full orchestra. A great descent of the horns and trumpets promises a triumphant end. But not yet; by sudden modulation the movement's most thrilling music is sounded. Mahler composed nothing more glowing, more proudly musical than this:

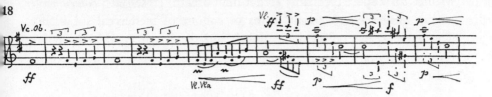

The counterpoint is rich, springy, proud and happy—a period of joy in work, unburdened. A rare moment in Mahler's creative life. Merely to look at the score at this point is stimulating, making one's musical senses to glow. I cannot refrain from quoting a few bars of the first violin's part-writing to the above example, if only for the pleasure of writing down the notes:

For nearly thirty bars the rapture goes on, the trombones coming in with the descending first four notes of the *Giocosa* melody, and the trumpet foretelling the chorale consummation (but we are not there yet):

But the fugue is far from exhausted. Frankly, a sticky patch has to be negotiated, with many fanfares of the persistent interval of a fourth. Mahler for a space (probably to get new breath) lapses into *Kapellmeister* music, until the movement seems in danger of ineffectual subsidence. The fugue ceases on an organ point, and the basses rumble the falling *Giocosa* notes in a dark abyss of gloom. Feeble wood-wind echoes of the Adagietto:

21

A recovery of purpose and attention to the movement's shape and destination is acclaimed in the nick of time by the familiar horn-call:

22

The Adagietto theme leads the way now, confidently, full swing. A delicious flick of the flutes, oboes and clarinets—never repeated—tells of Mahler's relish of his own art in this cornucopia of a Finale. Every instrument is vitally active and slightly but inspiringly crazy: higher and higher the leaps, with the fugue in headlong unison. The chorale, the consummation of the second movement's finale, declares the glory of man's effort and will. It is not a chorale telling of a religious faith. It is a Mahler affirmation of self-mastery; also it is a Mahlerian symphonic peroration, which caused him much trouble to get right instrumentally. As usual, he protests rather much; none the less this last movement is a wonderful apotheosis of the preceding parts—a symphonic world spinning and thundering away, stopped in its course only by a typical Mahler blow of dismissal.

In the coda to the chorale, Mahler assembles the movement's main introductory material—that is, the themes heard in the opening twenty bars or so; but the pace and scurry of notes defeat the ear's efforts at recognition. On paper, reduced to short score, the eye identifies at once:

My exploration (on paper) of this colossal symphony leaves me with a feeling of having conveyed to my readers the bare outlines. The symphony is a work of genius; it is Mahler's greatest contribution to symphonic music *proper* and 'absolute'. He attained a deeper, more inward tone and form in his Ninth Symphony, no doubt; but never again did he compose as exultantly, as abundantly, as comprehensively, as variously, as in the Fifth. The Sixth and Seventh Symphonies are, I think, less consistently masterful, and more contrived. They served as bridge passages to the Mahler of the Eighth and Ninth Symphonies and *Das Lied von der Erde*: the Mahler who, while conceiving *Das Lied* and the Ninth Symphony wrote, 'I have been going through so many experiences . . . that I can hardly discuss them . . . I see everything in such a new light and am in such continuous fluctuation—I shouldn't be surprised to discover that I had acquired a new body (as Faust does in the final scene).' The Fifth Symphony, Bruno Walter has written, is 'a masterpiece that shows its composer at the zenith of his life, his powers and his craft'. At the zenith of his craft—true. His 'powers' came later to finer and subtler texture. But in no other symphony did Mahler tell the world more convincingly that he was a musician than in the Fifth—'Ich bin Musiker'. Did not a 'programme', behind the tonal scenes, so to say, direct and inspire the Fifth Symphony? Only in the way that Beethoven was directed and inspired in his shaping of the *Eroica*. A 'programme' may be said to have dictated the musical *style*, the tone, the shaping, the tonal nuance and the dynamics. The scaffolding is discarded as soon as the edifice is up. There is no evidence now that a scaffolding has been used at all. Mahler's Fifth Symphony is one of the seven wonders of the symphonic world—and since it was composed sixty years ago, countless musicians, living full, active and lengthy lives in music, have died and never heard a note of it.

END OF VOLUME I

BIBLIOGRAPHY

Bekker, Paul: *Mahlers Sinfonien* (Schuster & Loeffler, Berlin, 1921)

Bauer-Lechner, Natalie: *Erinnerungen an Gustav Mahler* (Tal Verlag, Vienna, 1923)

Langford, Samuel: *Music Criticisms* (Oxford University Press, 1926)

Mahler, Alma: *Gustav Mahler, Erinnerungen und Briefe* (Albert de Lange, Amsterdam, 1940) English edition, *Memoirs and Letters* (John Murray Ltd., 1946)

Mitchell, Donald: *Gustav Mahler, The Early Years* (Barrie & Rockcliff, 1958)

Newlin, Dika: *Bruckner, Mahler, Schönberg* (New York, 1947)

Redlich, H. F.: *Bruckner and Mahler* (J. M. Dent & Sons Ltd., 1955)

Specht, Richard: *Gustav Mahler* (Schuster & Loeffler, Berlin, 1913)

Stefan, Paul: *Gustav Mahler* (Munich, 1910; English translation, G. Schirmer, New York, 1913)

Stein, Erwin: *Orpheus in New Guises* (London, Rockcliff, 1953)

Walter, Bruno: *Gustav Mahler* (Hamish Hamilton, 1958)

Chord and Discord: publication of the Bruckner Society of America